Tourism Management

Dr.S. Jeyashree

Associate Professor and Head

Department of Business Administration

Dr. Umayal Ramanathan College for Women, Karaikudi

Published by

Tourism Management

ISBN 978-93-85477-10-2

Author

Dr.S. Jeyashree

Bonfring
309, 2nd Floor, 5th Street Extension, Gandhipuram,
Coimbatore-641 012.
Tamilnadu, India.
E-mail: info@bonfring.org
Website: www.bonfring.org
Phone: 0422-3928700

Preface

Tourism is one of the fastest growing industries in the world; its ever increasing demand and provisions for relaxation and peaceful environment makes it one of the most important industries. Tourism, as such, has the capacity to transform the entire society and bring foreign wealth through the easiest way. Keeping this in mind, the book has been designed to serve the purpose of taking tourism studies to newer heights.

The book is specially designed to meet needs of the students of BBA and it is hoped that all those genuinely interested in tourism will find this book quite useful.

The object of this book is to set out the basic concepts of tourism in a simple language. An attempt has been made to present the concept as briefly and concisely as possible without sacrificing essential features.

Syllabus

UNIT I

History of Travel & Tourism, Ancient, Medeival & Contemporary Periods, Tourism, Definition, Forms, Motivation for Travel, Barriers to travel, Tourism Product, Travel Industry Network.

UNIT II

International Tourism, Top Tourism promoting Countries, Major destinations, Spending & earnings by different countries & other details, Domestic tourism, Indian tourism, Tourist attractions, Preferred places, Historical past, Culture, Seasonality, Foreign Exchange Earnings, profile of Visitors, Factors influencing tourism development, Social, Economic & Environmental impact on tourism.

UNIT III

Tourism & the state, National Tourism Administration (NTA), Comparative study of NTAs of various countries, Activities of Department of Tourism, Indian Tourism Development Corporation (ITDC), State Tourism Development Corporation (STDCs), Tourism Planning, Need for Planning, Process of Planning.

UNIT IV

Surface Transport, Airline Industry, Travel Agents, Functions, Automation in Travel industry, Computerised Reservation System (CRS), Importance of CRS for travel agents, World Tourism Organisation (WTO), International Air Transport Association.

Hotel Industry, Types of Tourist accommodation, management system of hotels, Franchise, Management Contract, Referral System, Hotel Industry in India, Finance Concessions & incentives given by government, major hotel chains of India, Tourism Promotion, Role & Importance, Advertising & Publicity.

<table>
<tr><th>Unit</th><th>Contents</th><th>Page No</th></tr>
</table>

<h1 align="center">Unit-I</h1>

History of Travel & Tourism

Tourism is a basic and most desirable human activity deserving the praise and encouragement of all people and all governments. It is an industry concerned with attracting people to a destination, transporting them there, housing, feeding and entertaining them upon arrival and returning them to their homes. A quarter of a century ago, travel was the privilege of a few rich, affluent and adventurous people. Today, with the rise in the standard of living of people in several developed and developing countries along with fast technological revolution in transportation industry, overseas holidays are within the reach of middle and working class. Travel, today, is sold like any normal consumer product through retail outlets, wholesalers, and even department stores of many countries. More and more people with small incomes are making overseas travel possible.

The history of tourism developed mainly through indirect sources in the early period. In India, in the early days of agricultural abundance, export of cash crops created an important trade link. Manufacture of iron-ore into steel for weaponry was another important item of trade by the later Vedic period. Tools and textiles were other renowned Indian products. Contemporary Greek and Hebrew scholars have noted the wonder of India and her fabled wealth. Owing to the predominance of trade routes over – land crossing between Asia and Europe, trade tours were an important development in this period.

In the early days, pilgrimage or pilgrim travel assumed great importance. Ashoka the great, travelled a great deal in his eagerness to spread the doctrines of Buddha. Throughout his travels, from Pataliputra to Lumbini on to Kapilavastu and Sarnath and finally to Gaya, Emperor Ashoka had special memorials set up at each spot and also rest houses where travellers could rest. Trees were planted along the road sides so that the traveller would be protected from the harsh sun shine. Harsha was another great emperor who gently influenced by the Buddhist scriptures, built institutions and Dharamsalas for the travellers. Rest houses were built in towns and villages. A number of monasteries were also built for the pilgrims. This shows that travel facilities were much improved and travel was not a cumbersome experience.

Brahmin villages evolved into centers of learning attracting scholars. At this time the Buddhist Sanga established the tradition of pilgrimage, when monks went from village to village and court preaching the value of the middle-path. Rest houses were provided for the travellers. Monastries also attracted the monks, middlemen and laymen.

The Arthashastra reflects the protection given to merchants and their high status in the Indian society. Insurance and safe passage for goods, regulation of prices, weights and measures and the use of gold, silver and copper as rates of exchange also indicate a well-developed mode of trade and travel.

The Arthashastra also reveals the importance of the travel infrastructure for the state, classification of routes and types of vehicles. This is an indication that there was a well-developed mode of travel in India for the military, the commercial traveller and the civilian. Travel on inland waterways was also under state protection and regulation. In cities, bazaars provided access to goods brought from the hinterland. Travellers were accommodated in overnight places of stay, known as series at the city gates where all services were provided to them. State regulations insisted on travellers carrying with them a note for safe passage from one territory to the other. Entertainment and dancing halls were allowed, gambling was licensed and was a source of income for the state.

In ancient times people travelled for the purpose of war, religious pilgrimage and trading. From the third century the ancient Greeks, for example, travelled to visit the sites of their gods and to visit the temples.

During the Roman Empire, citizens of Rome travelled freely to those countries their armies had conquered, using their own currency and not having to worry about border restrictions.

The Romans built long straight roads along which their armies could march and goods could be transported .The Romans established trade and created leisure facilities such as spas - the most famous example in this country is the Roman spa in Bath.

With the fall of the Roman Empire around 400AD, and for a period after, only the most adventurous or those involved in international trade travelled abroad.

In the middle Ages people seldom travelled, apart from going on pilgrimage, however there were holidays. Most transport was by foot or on horseback, though some people could afford a wagon.

In the early 1600s the sprung coach was introduced. This was more comfortable but could only be afforded by the very rich.

In the early seventeenth century wealthy young men were travelling across Europe on the Grand Tour, spending as long as a year visiting the capitals of Europe, as part of their education.

In the early seventeenth century wealthy young men were travelling across Europe on the Grand Tour, spending as long as a year visiting the capitals of Europe, as part of their education.

Another development in travel at this time was the taking of 'a cure' by the wealthy, who visited the various spa towns to take the waters, which were reputed to provide a cure for a range of ailments.

By 1815, tarmac had been developed for use as a road surface, which led to further developments in the road system in the UK and to an increase in the movement of people and vehicles.

The development of the railways increased the opportunity for travel. With the opening of the first rail services in 1825, people could travel longer distances for excursions to the seaside.

People had a strong desire for travel to escape the dreary working and living conditions of the factories and towns that emerged during the industrial revolution of the nineteenth century.

The development of transport made this possible. However, whatever holiday's factory workers took, they were not paid during them. Paid holidays were not introduced until 1938.

The history of tourism can be divided into 6 different stages as follow:

i. **Roman Empire Period:** During the Roman Empire period (from about 27 BC to AD 476), travel developed for military, trade and political reasons, as well as for communication of messages from the central government to its distant territories. Travel was also necessary for the artisans and architects "imported" to design and construct the great palaces and tombs. In ancient Greece, people traveled to Olympic Games. Both the participants and spectators required accommodations and food services. Wealthy Romans, in ancient times, traveled to seaside resorts in Greece and Egypt for sightseeing purpose.

ii. **Middle Age Period:** During the Middle Age (from about AD 500 to 1400), there was a growth of travel for religious reasons. It had become an organized phenomenon for pilgrims to visit their "holy land", such as Muslims to Mecca, and Christians to Jerusalem and Rome.

iii.   **16th Century:** In the 16th century, the growth in England's trade and commerce led to the rise of a new type of tourists - those traveled to broaden their own experience and knowledge.

iv.   **17th Century:** In the 17th century, the sons and daughters of the British aristocracy traveled throughout Europe (such as Italy, Germany and France) for periods of time, usually 2 or 3 years, to improve their knowledge. This was known as the Grand Tour, which became a necessary part of the training of future administrators and political leaders.

v.   **Industrial Revolution Period:** The Industrial Revolution (from about AD 1750 to 1850) in Europe created the base for mass tourism. This period turned most people away from basic agriculture into the town/factory and urban way of life. As a result, there was a rapid growth of the wealth and education level of the middle class, as well as an increase of leisure time and a demand for holiday tourism activities. At that time, travel for health became important when the rich and fashionable Europeans began to visit the spa towns (such as Bath in England and Baden - Baden in Germany) and seaside resorts in England (such as Scarborough, Margate and Brighton).

vi.   **19th to 20th Centuries:** In the 19th and 20th centuries, the social and technological changes have had an immense impact on tourism. Great advances in science and technology made possible the invention of rapid, safe and relatively cheap forms of transport: the railways were invented in the 19th century and the passenger aircraft in the 20th century. World War II (AD 1939-1945) was also the impetus for dramatic improvements in communication and air transportation, which made travel much easier today than in earlier times.

1980s

The 1980s were called the boom years. Business and leisure travel expanded very rapidly. The baby-boomers were coming of age and had the money to spend. These travellers were looking for a variety of tourism products from exciting vacation options such as adventure travel, ecotourism and luxurious travel.

There was not only a significant expansion in the travel market but also in tourist destinations. The fall of the Berlin Wall in Germany in 1989 signified the doom of communism in Europe. Countries such as Russia and the Czech Republic became new tourist destinations both for vacation and business travellers.

1990s

The Aviation Industry was facing high operational costs, including wage, oil prices, handling fee of Central Reservation System (CRS), landing charge of the air crafts and advertising fee etc. During this decade, CRS also marched towards more sophisticated technology. It became possible for agents to book a huge inventory of tourism products, such as hotels, car rentals, cruises, rail passes, and theatre tickets from the CRS.

The introduction of "ticketless traveling" (electronic ticket) brings benefits to the airlines by cutting the amount of paperwork and cost of tickets. At the same time, passengers do not have to worry about carrying or losing tickets. Although, electronic ticketing does not bypass the travel agents as intermediaries, it makes it easier for the airline to deal directly with consumers.

The advance in technology also allows the airlines and other travel suppliers to sell directly to travellers through the Internet and interactive kiosks at airports. The kiosks at the airport usually sell hotel accommodation, transfer tickets such as bus tickets between airport and downtown areas and coach tickets from one city to another.

Travellers can now log on to the Internet easily reach for travel information, book a simple ticket or hotel room through their personal computer at home. There are thousands of new destinations, tour products and discounted airfares for travellers to choose from.

Definition of Tourism

Tourism means the temporary short-term movement of people to destinations outside the places where they normally live and work, as well as their activities during their stay at these destinations. It should be noted that all tourism should have some travel, but not all travel is tourism.

'Tourism comprises the activities of persons travelling to and staying in places outside their usual environment for not more than one consecutive year for leisure, business and other purposes.'

Types and Forms of Tourism

Tourism is the movement of the tourists from one place to another place. It is the temporary short-term movement of people to destinations outside the place where they normally live &work includes the activities they indulge in at the destination as well as all facilities and services specially created to meet their needs. Tourism does not only mean traveling to a particular destination but also includes all activities undertaken during the stay.

It includes day visits & excursions. The movement can be in your country or the tourists can also travel to the foreign destinations for the tourism purpose.

On this basis tourism can be divided into

i. Domestic Tourism

ii. International Tourism

Tourism is basically travelling to another destination for the purposes of recreation, leisure, or business.

A person who travels to a destination and stays outside of where they usually live for more than 24 hours but less than one year is recognized as a tourist by the World Tourism Organization.

The type of tourism depends on the reason for travel. Travel can be to destinations that are **domestic** or **international**.

Domestic tourism involves residents travelling only within their country.

Inbound and Outbound tourism both describe types of international tourism.

Inbound tourism involves non-residents travelling within a country.

Outbound tourism, involves residents travelling within another country.

i. *Leisure Tourism*

Tourists may travel to experience a change in climate and place and learn something new, enjoy pleasant scenery, or to know more about the culture of a destination. Tourists, who seek break from the stress of day to day life, devote their holiday to rest and relaxation, refresh themselves. These tourists prefer to stay in some quiet and relaxed destination preferably at a hill resort, beach resort or island resort.

ii. *Cultural Tourism*

It is also called as heritage tourism. People are curious to know about foreign lands and their cultures. Culture is most important factors which attracts tourists to a destination.

- Cultural tourism gives insight to
- Way of life of the people of distant land
- Dress, jewelry, dance, music, architecture
- Customs and traditions

- Fairs and festivals
- Religions
- Culinary delights

iii. *Religious Tourism*

It is also called as Pilgrimage tourism/Spiritual tourism. It is a form of tourism, where people travel individually or in groups for pilgrimage. The world's largest form of mass religious tourism takes place at the annual Hajj pilgrimage in Mecca, Saudi Arabia. Modern religious tourists are more able to visit holy cities and holy sites around the world. The most famous holy cities are Jerusalem, Mecca and Varanasi.

iv. *Family Tourism*

Family tourism involves the family unit and their participation in diverse forms of tourism activity. This includes visiting one's relatives and friends for interpersonal reasons. Many people in India travel for visiting their friends and relatives. While visiting friends or relatives, people also visit tourists' attractions in and around the city.

v. *Health Tourism*

Health tourism is also called as Medical tourism. People have been travelling for centuries to improve and rebuild their health and stamina. Today, many people travel great distances to exotic locations or health care facilities in faraway countries, in search of medical treatment and care. Medical tourism is an age-old concept that has gained popularity in the recent times. Many developing countries are emerging as hot medical tourism destinations capitalizing on low cost advantages. Many hospitals have specially designed packages including resorts facilities.

Thus health tourism covers one or more of the following aspects:

- Change of climate
- Alternative therapy-Ayruvedic treatment, hot Sulphur springs, Naturopathy and art of living
- Medical treatment

vi.   *Sports Tourism*

Sports Tourism refers to travel which involves either viewing or participating in a sporting event staying apart from their usual environment. Sport tourism is a fast growing sector of the global travel industry. Sports tourism refers to people travelling to participate in a competitive sport event. Normally these kinds of events are the motivators that attract visitors to visit the events like Olympic Games, FIFA World Cup.

vii.   *Educational Tourism*

Educational tourism developed, because of the growing popularity of teaching and learning of knowledge and the enhancing of technical competency outside of the classroom environment. In educational tourism, the main focus of the tour visiting another country to learn about the culture, such as in Student Exchange Programs and Study Tours, organizing specialized lectures of the eminent personalities and for research. Image.

viii.   *Business Tourism*

The business traveler's main motive for travel is work. Tourists visit a particular destination for various reasons pertaining to his/her work such as attending a business meeting, conferences, conventions selling products, meeting clients. Business tourism is popularly called as MICE (Meetings, incentives, conferences, and exhibitions) tourism.

Travel Motivation

A motivation is a wish that prompts people to take action, work hard to achieve a goal, and satisfy a certain kind of need. For example, when a person is hungry and there is a need to appease his or her hunger, a motivation to search for food is formed. Therefore, people's activities of all kinds are driven by their motivations, and they govern people's actions.

Travellers are motivated to satisfy a need, and they have a perception of what will satisfy their need. At the same time, travellers have a perception of the attractions of the destination and whether the attractions satisfy their needs. If both sides are agreed, travellers are motivated to visit that destination.

The Push and Pull Theory

In 1977, Dann, a U.S. academic, put forward the push-pull theory of travel motivations. He considered that travel behaviour was influenced by both push factors and pull factors.

People travel because they are "pushed" into making travel decisions by internal, psychological forces, and "pulled" by the external forces of the destination attributes.

Push Factors

These are internal or intangible factors that lead to the formation of travel desires among potential tourists. Anything that can relieve and fulfill tourists' desires can thus become a focus or target. In short, these are socio-psychological factors that motivate or create a desire to satisfy a need to travel. Therefore, under the influence of push factors, tourists who go travelling do not necessarily have specific, clear choices.

For example, tourists who hope to improve their relationships with family members don't really care where they go, the key is to spend quality time together with family.

Pull Factors

These are factors that influence where tourists go travelling. Pull factors are the attractiveness or "drawing power" of the destination as perceived by the traveler, and they are likely help traveler to make an actual destination choice. Tourists form pull-type travel motivations on the basis of their perception, expectation and knowledge of destinations. Because of this, tourists who go travelling under the influence of pull factors always have a clear destination.

For example, a newly married couple may go to the sunshine and beaches of the Maldives to testify to their love, and will not choose other travel destinations.

Push & Pull Motives

"Push & Pull factors have been widely accepted to explain tourist behaviour and travel motivations" (Crompton, 1979; Uysal& Hagen, 1993; as cited in Chan & Baum, 2007, pg.359). Dann (1997) simply explains push factors as the motive that drives a tourist away from home and pull factors as the motives in which drive a tourist towards a destination. However with more complexity the push factors encouraging a person to travel are the socio-psychological needs of a person (Yoon &Uysal, 2005) and the pull factors are the motivations arousing a person to visit a particular destination (Buhalis, 2003; Flucker& Turner; as cited in Chan & Baum, 2007). Crompton (1979) distinguishes 7 socio-psychological motives: escape from a perceived mundane environment, exploration and evaluation of self, relaxation, prestige, regression, enhancement of kinship relationships and facilitation of social interaction; and 2 cultural motives: novelty and education.

Gray (1970) however defines the same push and pull motives as 'sunlust' and 'wanderlust'. Sunlust describes those "vacations in which are motivated by the desire to experience different or better amenities for a specific purpose than are available in the environment in which one normally lives" (Crompton, 1977, p. 410). And alternative wanderlust is described as the "basic trait in human nature that causes some individuals to want to leave things with which they are familiar and to go and see at first hand different existing cultures and places" (Crompton, 1977, p. 410).

Factors that Influence Travel Motivations and Actions

Factors that influence one's travel motivations and decisions can be categorized into two different aspects: internal factors and external factors.

Internal Factors (Individual Factors)

Economic Capacity

Economic capacity is the basis on which all needs are formed. Because travel is a kind of consumer behaviour, the ability to pay the various types of charges involved is of course necessary. When a person's economic income can only support his or her basic living needs, he or she will not form a motivation to go travelling. As an economy develops, in countries and regions where citizens' income increases, the tourism industry becomes more developed, and the number of people who go travelling climbs, or drops when the opposite applies.

Spare Time

Spare time refers to the time that people can freely allocate to taking part in pastimes and entertainment or anything else they enjoy participating in after their daily work, study, living and other compulsory time commitments. Travel necessarily takes up a certain amount of time, and if a person cannot get away from official business or family matters and has no spare time to freely allocate and set aside for his or her own pastimes, he or she cannot go travelling. Therefore, spare time is an important condition for the realization of travel activities.

Sex, Age and Physical Condition

Compared with females, males are psychologically more proactive, risk-tolerant and willing to seek novelty, which spurs them to form the desire to go travelling more easily than females. Young people's need to have curious minds and a psychological need to outdo others, as well as a great ability to accept new things. Therefore, when compared with other people, their travel motivations are less affected or limited by reality.

Psychological Factors

Travel motivations are a form of individual psychological activity, and are inevitably influenced by various aspects such as individual interests, hobbies, profession, attitude to life, understanding of the surrounding environment, level of education, and family.

External Factors (External Environmental Conditions)

Overall Development of the Tourism Industry

It is only when the economy of a country or region is developed that it will have enough resources to improve and construct travel facilities, develop tourist attractions and promote transport development. Road transport facilities, accommodation, catering, and service standards at a destination are important factors in the tourists' choice of destination, and also affect their formation of travel motivations to a large degree, especially for tourists with relatively high hospitality expectations.

Group, Family and Social Atmosphere

Group or social pressure can also influence people's travel motivations. For example, travel activities organized by enterprises, or travel awards, etc. encourage people to form their own travel motivations involuntarily, and travel activities subsequently take place.

Social surroundings can also influence people's travel motivations. Colleagues', friends' and relatives' travel behaviour and travel experiences can always influence others, or lead to the formation of a comparative psychology, making people form identical travel motivations, and leading to the formation of a kind of imitative travel behaviour.

Barriers to Travel

Traveling is an amazing adventure. Whether you're taking a road trip to a national park or flying across the globe to see the pyramids of Egypt, traveling truly provides endless opportunities for relaxation, adventure, and learning. However, many individuals face specific obstacles that make traveling difficult. Luckily, many of these common barriers can be minimized or even eliminated.

Cost: Many individuals feel that they cannot travel simply because it costs too much. Yes, depending on the location and duration of the trip, traveling can become very expensive. Generally, flights and accommodations tend to affect the wallet the most. However, even if you do not have an unlimited discretionary income, it is still possible to travel.

Time: Another common barrier that holds individuals back from traveling is their perceived lack of free time to do so. Yes, everyone is busy! However, even with just a long weekend, you can do a lot.

No Companion to Travel With: Many people indicate that they choose not to travel because they have no one to travel with. Even if you do not have friends or family members who enjoy or care to travel, it is not impossible to find other individuals like yourself who are eager to get out there but really have no one to join them. Luckily, there are various websites, such as **TravBuddy.com** that allow you to find other people who are traveling to the same destinations as you. A second option is to go to your local travel agency and sign up for a group trip. Regardless of the route, finding a traveling buddy who is just as enthusiastic about traveling as you are is completely possible.

Lack of Knowledge: It is sad to think that there are some people who decide to never travel because they aren't aware of what's out there. In this instance, a little knowledge can go a long way. If you have never traveled in the past and have never even considered it, do some research on what is out there. You might be amazed to find what the world has to offer.

Fear of the Unknown and Unfamiliar: Yes, traveling will force you to step outside your comfort zone. You will have to interact with new people, navigate new towns and cities, and try to overcome culture shock at certain destinations. However, these are not experiences that should be looked down upon, feared, or dreaded. Traveling is an awesome opportunity and fear isn't going to get you anywhere. While although the first few days of your trip may be intimidating and overwhelming, you will eventually become more comfortable in the new locale. After traveling to different destinations often, the whole process will really become second nature. You will learn how to acclimate yourself to the area and be a travel warrior in no time!

Tourism Product

The tourism product is composite in nature. It includes what the tourist purchases, sees, experiences and feels from the time he/she leaves home until he/she returns. They may be in the forms of

1. Journey to and from the destination.
2. Things purchased including accommodation, food, beverages, souvenirs, amusement and entertainment.
3. Experiences and expectations which are not purchased.
4. The price of tour.

Characteristics of Tourism Product

1. Tourism products are available at the destination. They cannot be moved outside the destination. So the tourist has to be present at the destination for consumption of tourism products.

2. Tourism products cannot be brought back with the tourist to his/her home. Only memories of the tourism products in form of photographs, videos can be with the tourist.

3. Tourism products cannot be stored. Out of 100 seats there are 80 seats occupied in an airplane from New Delhi to Mumbai, then there is loss of revenue for 20 seats for that flight. And this loss can never be recovered.

4. Tourism products cannot be owned by the tourist. If you visit TajMahal by purchasing the entry ticket, it does not mean you own TajMahal.

5. Tourism products have to be purchased and then consumed by the buyer at the destination. If one has to enjoy beaches of Goa, then one has to make booking for hotel, transportation etc by making payment. Then has to go to Goa and enjoy the beaches. It cannot be like you can test drive various cars before purchasing one.

6. Tourism products are made available by people. So they are highly dependent on people who are providing it. If a guide is unable to give you good commentary on Red Fort then your visit to Red Fort will not be successful.

7. Tourism products are highly dependent upon the experience of the tourist. So it becomes difficult to measure the level of product quality.

Classification of Tourism Product

Natural tourism products- Beaches, islands, mountains, hills, desert, wildlife (flora and fauna), caves, glaciers, lakes, waterfalls, rivers. Examples: palm fringed beaches of Goa, snow cappedountains in Kashmir, the flora and fauna of Kaziranga National Park in Assam, Dudhsagar fall in Goa, Thar Desert in Jaisalmer etc. Beach in Goa Kaziranga National Park

Man made tourism products- The manmade tourism products are those which are built by humans. There can be manmade tourism products which are purposely built for tourists. They can be museums, casinos, theme parks. There are manmade attractions which are not originally designed to attract tourists. They are forts, palaces, temples etc. The manmade attractions also include customs and traditions of a destination. Folk dance, classical dance, music, handicrafts, fairs and festivals etc are other manmade attractions. Examples: TajMahal, Red Fort, India Gate, Lothal in Gujarat is an important archaeological Indus Valley Site;

National Museum in New Delhi, Bhangra of Punjab, Madhubani paintings of Bihar, Brass work of Muradabad etc. TajMahal Folk Dance of Punjab Bhangra Site based tourism products- When attraction is a place or site then it is site based tourism product. Site of TajMahal, sunset at Kanyakumari etc. Sunset at Kanyakumari Event based tourism product-Events attract tourists as spectator and also as participants in the events, sometimes both. Kite flying in Ahmadabad attracts tourist both as spectators and participants. Tourists can be spectators for events like Olympics, Khajuraho dance festival. Holi festival

Travel Industry Network

- The tourism industry of India is economically important and is growing rapidly. The World Travel & Tourism Council calculated that tourism generated INR6.4 trillion or 6.6% of the nation's GDP in 2012. It supported 39.5 million jobs, 7.7% of its total employment. The sector is predicted to grow at an average annual rate of 7.9% from 2013 to 2023. This gives India the third rank among countries with the fastest growing tourism industries over the next decade. India has a large medical tourism sector which is expected to grow at an estimated rate of 30% annually to reach about 95 billion by 2015.

- According to provisional statistics 7.42 million foreign tourists arrived in India in 2014, an increase of 7.4% from 6.96 million in 2013. This ranks India as the 38th country in the world in terms of foreign tourist arrivals. Domestic tourist visits to all states and Union Territories numbered 1,036.35 million in 2012, an increase of 16.5% from 2011

- The most represented countries are the United States (16%) and the United Kingdom (12.6%). In 2011, Maharashtra, Tamil Nadu and Delhi were the most popular states for foreign tourists. Domestic tourists visited the states Uttar Pradesh, Andhra Pradesh and Tamil Nadu most frequently. Chennai, Delhi, Mumbai and Agra have been the four most visited cities of India by foreign tourists during the year 2011. Worldwide, Chennai is ranked 38 by the number of foreign tourists, while Mumbai is ranked at 50, Delhi at 52 and Agra at 66 and Kolkata at 99.

- The Travel & Tourism Competitiveness Report 2013 ranks India 65th out of 144 countries overall. The report ranks the price competitiveness of India's tourism sector 20th out of 144 countries.

- It mentions that India has quite good air transport (ranked 39th), particularly given the country's stage of development, and reasonable ground transport infrastructure (ranked 42nd). Some other aspects of its tourism infrastructure remain somewhat underdeveloped however. The World Tourism Organization reported that India's receipts from tourism during 2012 ranked 16th in the world, and 7th among Asian and Pacific countries.

- The Ministry of Tourism designs national policies for the development and promotion of tourism. In the process, the Ministry consults and collaborates with other stakeholders in the sector including various Central Ministries/agencies, state governments, Union Territories and the representatives of the private sector. Concerted efforts are being made to promote new forms of tourism such as rural, cruise, medical and eco-tourism. The Ministry also maintains the Incredible India campaign.
- India's rich history and its cultural and geographical diversity make its international tourism appeal large and diverse. It presents heritage and cultural tourism along with medical, business, educational and sports tourism.

Unit-II

International Tourism

An international tourist crosses the boundaries of many countries, uses different currencies, faces different languages and meets different types of people. Usually international tourism involves longer distances although crossing small countries or travelling in the neighborhood of international borders may involve short distances. An international tourist has been defined as a person visiting other country and staying at least for 24 hours and maximum for 6 months and the main purpose of his visit is other than the exercise of an activity related to work at earnings or establishment of residence in the country visited. Such person must carry a valid passport, visa, health certificates, amount of currency carrying and other essential information required by authorities of the concerned country from time to time.

Domestic Tourism

It is concerned with travelling within the country. It does not need a passport and visa or conversion of one currency into another. Domestic tourism has greater scope in countries of large dimensions such as India as compared to smaller countries. From a geographical viewpoint, domestic tourism may range from local excursion, regional trips to national level travels. A domestic tourist has been defined as a person who travels within the country to a place other than his normal place of residence and stays at hotels or other such establishments run on commercial basis like youth hostels, guest hostels, dharmashala, circuit houses etc are stays with friends and relatives and visits the nplaces of attraction or pilgrimages for a duration of not less than 24 hours and maximum of 6 months. Such persons do not require any document like passport or visa etc.

Difference between Domestic Tourism and International Tourism

Table 1: Difference between Domestic Tourism and International Tourism

Domestic Tourism	*International Tourism*
Earnings from home Tourism cannot claim any extra weightage in Investment planning.	Earnings from International Tourism in the form of tourism exchange claim extra weightage Investment planning.
Demand for have tourism can easily be regulated.	It is not possible regulate the demand for international tourism.
The Demand for home tourism reflects the international distribution in incomes.	It does not reflect the International Distribution in Income.

Tourism Promotion

Tourism promotion means stimulating sales through dissemination of information. It means trying to encourage actual and potential customers to travel.

Objectives

1. To make the tourist products widely known.
2. To make it very attractive in order to encourage many people to try it.
3. To make the message attractive without being dishonest.

Top Tourism Promoting Countries

Singapore

Singapore is one of the great cities of the world, with its blend of Asian and European cultures Graceful colonial buildings co-exist alongside centuries-old street markets and modern high-rises. Though the government can be strict with residents and visitors who misbehave, travelers who follow the rules can't help but be fascinated by this multi-cultural city. In fact, Singapore is one of the easiest and most comfortable countries to navigate in Southeast Asia. Top tourist attractions in Singapore are Marina Bay Sands, Singapore Flyer, Buddha Tooth Relic Temple, Night Safari, Singapore Botanic Garden, Gardens By The Bay, Raffles Hotel, Clarke Quay, Resorts World Sentose, Orchard Road

Paris

As the capital city of France, Paris has endured as an important city for more than 2,000 years. Often called by nicknames like the "city of love" and "city of lights," Paris is today one of the world's leading centers for business, fashion, entertainment, art and culture. Paris offers the largest concentration of tourist attractions in France, and possibly in Europe. Besides some of the world's most famous musuems, it has a vibrant historic city centre, a beautiful river scape, an extensive range of historic monuments, including cathedrals, chapels and palaces, plus one of the most famous nightlife scenes in the world. Paris is also famous for its cafés and restaurants, its theatres and cinemas, and its general ambiance. Just the mere mention of Paris conjures up images of the city's world famous landmarks, museums and cathedrals. The top tourist attractions in Paris are Place De La Concorde, Sainte-Chapella, Centre Pompidou, MuseeD'orsay, Jardin Du Luxembourg, Sacre-Coeur, Notre Dame De Paris,Arc De Triomphe, Louvre, Eiffle Tower.

London

London is one of the most popular destinations in the world, having welcomed a record breaking 17.4 million visitors alone in 2014! It's no surprise, as the city offers a wide range of historic attractions, top museums, art galleries, tours and experiences for every one of all ages to enjoy.

One of the most popular historic attractions in London is the **Tower of London** which dates back to the Norman Conquest in 1066. One of the best museums is **Churchill War Rooms** dedicated to Britain's former Prime Minister, Winston Churchill, and his efforts and influences during WWII. Other fascinating museums to discover more about London is the **Guards Museum**, **Charles Dickens Museum**, **Design Museum London** and the **London Transport Museum**.

New York

Tourism in New York City serves over 56 million foreign and American tourists each year including day-trippers. Major destinations include the Empire State Building, Ellis Island, Broadway theatre productions, museums such as the Metropolitan Museum of Art, and other tourist attractions including Central Park, Washington Square Park, Rockefeller Center, Times Square, the Bronx Zoo, Barclays Center, Coney Island, South Street Seaport, New York Botanical Garden, luxury shopping along Fifth and Madison Avenues, and events such as the Tribeca Film Festival, and free performances in Central Park at Summer stage and Delacorte Theater. The Statue of Liberty is a major tourist attraction and one of the most recognizable icons of the United States. Many New York City ethnic enclaves, such as Jackson Heights, Flushing, and Brighton Beachare major shopping destinations for first and second generation Americans up and down the East Coast.

Dubai

Tourism in Dubai, part of the United Arab Emirates, is an important part of the Dubai government's strategy to maintain the flow of foreign cash into the emirate. Dubai's lure for tourists is based mainly on shopping, but also on its possession of other ancient and modern attractions. This city of high-rises and shopping malls has transformed itself from a desert outpost to a destination du-jour, where people flock for sales bargains, sunshine and family fun. Dubai is famous for sightseeing attractions such as the **BurjKhalifa** (the world's tallest building) and shopping malls that come complete with mammoth aquariums and indoor ski slopes. But this city has many cultural highlights as well as all the glamorous modern add-ons.

Kaula Lumpur

The most popular and iconic attractions in Kuala Lumpur have come to define the city as a tourist destination-from the unmistakable outline of the Petronas Twin Towers to the colossal standing Buddha image found outside Batu Caves. However, Kuala Lumpur attractions comprise so much more for those who want to look deeper into this fascinating city. from the colorful Petaling Street market in Chinatown Kuala Lumpur and the famous Sultan Abdul Samad Building in the city's colonial quarter, to the indoor Aquaria KLCC oceanarium and Petrosains Art Gallery in Suria KLCC. There is a lot of greenery in Kuala Lumpur, with the Lake Gardens home to popular bird and deer parks.

Hong Kong

The tourism industry has been an important part of the economy of Hong Kong since it shifted to a service sector model in the late 1980s and early 90s. There has been a sharp increase of tourists from Mainland China, due to the introduction of the Individual Visit Scheme (IVS) in 2003.

Bangkok

Bangkok, the capital of Thailand, is one of the world's top tourist destination cities. MasterCard ranked Bangkok as the global top destination city by international visitor arrivals in its Global Destination Cities Index, with 15.98 million projected visitors in 2013. The city is ranked fourth in cross-border spending, with 14.3 billion dollars projected for 2013, after New York, Londo and Paris. Euromonitor International ranked Bangkok sixth in its Top City Destinations Ranking for 2011. Bangkok has also been named "World's Best City" by *Travel + Leisure* magazine's survey of its readers for three consecutive years since 2010.

Spain

Tourism in Spain is a major contributor to the national economic life, contributing 6.4% of Spain's GDP. Ever since the 1960s and 1970s, the country has been a popular destination for summer holidays, especially with the tourists from the UK, Germany, France, Ireland, Scandinavia, Italy and the Benelux. Spain has held strong position in world's tourism, being among the largest markets for holidays.

Spain ranks first among 141 countries in the Travel and Tourism Competitiveness Index published by the World Economic Forum in 2015.

Tourist destination is "a country, state, region, city or town which is marketed or markets itself as a place for tourists to visit."

A tourist destination is basically a travel destination that attracts large numbers of travelers, or tourists. Travelers may visit these destinations to see historical sites, natural wonders, or buildings. Some tourist attractions also have activities, such as rides or games, or unusual novelties. Souvenirs are often sold at these destinations, and many of these areas rely on the income generated by the travelers that visit.

Historical sites are often considered tourist destination. Monuments and battlegrounds can be considered historical tourist attractions. Gettysburg, Pennsylvania is a good example of a historical tourist destination. This town was the site of a pivotal battle during the American Civil War in 1863, and it is also the site of President Abraham Lincoln's famous Gettysburg address. Areas with beautiful or unusual natural creations can also be considered tourist destinations. Visitors to these areas are usually able to see amazing natural wonders, such as a waterfalls or canyons. For example, each year millions of tourists from all over the world visit Niagara Falls, a tourist destination located on the border of the United States and Canada. These magnificent waterfalls are considered to be one of the Seven Natural Wonders of the World.

World's Top 10 Tourism Destinations

The World Tourism Organization reports the following ten countries as the most visited in terms of the number of international travellers in 2014.

Rank	*Country*	*UN WTO Region* [21]	*International tourist arrivals (2014)*	*International tourist arrivals (2013)*	*Change (2013 to 2014) (%)*	*Change (2012 to 2013) (%)*
1	France	Europe	83.7 million	83.6 million	0.1	2.0
2	United States	North America	74.8 million	70.0 million	6.8	5.0
3	Spain	Europe	65.0 million	60.7 million	7.1	5.6
4	China	Asia	55.6 million	55.7 million	0.1	3.5
5	Italy	Europe	48.6 million	47.7 million	1.8	2.9
6	Turkey	Europe	39.8 million	37.8 million	5.3	5.9
7	Germany	Europe	33.0 million	31.5 million	4.6	3.7
8	United Kingdom	Europe	32.6 million	31.1 million	5.0	6.1
9	Russia	Europe	29.8 million	28.4 million	5.3	10.2
10	Mexico	North America	29.1 million	24.2 million	20.5	3.2

International Tourism Receipts

International tourism receipts grew to US$1.245 billion in 2014, corresponding to an increase in real terms of 3.7% from 2013.The World Tourism Organization reports the following countries as the top ten tourism earners for the year 2014, with the United States by far the top earner.

Rank	Country	UNWTO Region [21]	International tourism receipts (2014)[22]	International tourism receipts (2013)[23]	Change (2013 to2014) (%)	Change (2012 to2013) (%)
1	United States	North America	$177.2 billion	$172.9 billion	2.5	7.0
2	Spain	Europe	$65.2 billion	$62.6 billion	4.2	7.6
3	China	Asia	$56.9 billion	$51.7 billion	10.2	3.3
4	France	Europe	$55.4 billion	$56.7 billion	2.3	5.6
—	Macau, China	Asia	$50.8 billion	$51.8 billion	1.9	18.1
5	Italy	Europe	$45.5 billion	$43.9 billion	3.7	6.6
6	United Kingdom	Europe	$45.3 billion	$41.0 billion	10.3	12.1
7	Germany	Europe	$43.3 billion	$41.3 billion	5.0	8.2
8	Thailand	Asia	$38.4 billion	$41.8 billion	8.0	23.4
—	Hong Kong, China	Asia	$38.4 billion	$38.9 billion	1.4	17.7
9	Australia	Oceania	$32.0 billion	$31.2 billion	1.8	0.5
10	Turkey	Europe	$29.5 billion	$27.9 billion	3.7	4.1

International Tourism Expenditure

The World Tourism Organization reports the following countries as the top ten biggest spenders on international tourism for the year 2014.

Rank	Country	UNWTO Region [21]	International tourism expenditure (2014)[22]	International tourism expenditure (2013)[23]	Market Share (%)	Change (2013 to 2014) (%)
1	China	Asia	$164.9 billion	$128.6 billion	13.2	27.1
2	United States	North America	$110.8 billion	$104.1 billion	8.9	6.4
3	Germany	Europe	$92.2 billion	$91.4 billion	7.4	0.9
4	United Kingdom	Europe	$57.6 billion	$52.7 billion	4.6	3.8
5	Russia	Europe	$50.4 billion	$53.5 billion	4.0	13.7
6	France	Europe	$47.8 billion	$42.9 billion	3.8	11.3
7	Canada	North America	$33.8 billion	$35.2 billion	2.7	3.3
8	Italy	Europe	$28.8 billion	$27.0 billion	2.3	6.9
9	Australia	Oceania	$26.3 billion	$28.6 billion	2.1	1.7
10	Brazil	South America	$25.6 billion	$25.0 billion	2.1	11.7

Tourist Attraction

A **tourist attraction** is a place of interest where tourists visit, for natural or cultural value, historical significance, built beauty, offering leisure, adventure and amusement. A place that people visit for pleasure and interest, usually while they are on holiday. Tourist attractions are by definition anything that attracts tourists. Any site that appeals to people sufficiently to encourage them to travel there in order to visit it can be judged a visitor attraction. A tourist attraction is a system comprising three elements: a tourist or human element, a nucleus or central element, and a marker or informative element. A tourist attraction comes into existence when the three elements are connected.

The Elements of a Successful Tourist Attraction

1. **Resource Elements**: a successful tourist attraction needs a striking and/or distinctive physical or cultural resource as its core.
2. **Public Conceptions/Understanding**: the successful tourist attraction should be readily appreciated by the public or offer interpretive facilities so that the public may understand and appreciate the resource.
3. **Visitor Activities**: the successful tourist attraction will provide scope for visitor experience and activities which are responsible, accessible and excite public imagination
4. **Inviolate Belt**: the successful tourist attraction will be presented in a context which preserves the resource and enables the visitor to appreciate and reflect on the resource qualities.
5. **Services Zone**: the successful tourist attraction will provide visitor services (toilets, shopping, etc.) but not to the detriment of the resource
6. **Price**: The successful tourist attraction will be priced to reflect the quality of the resource and its management, visitors" length of stay and a healthily return on public or private investment.

Tourist Destinations in India

Agra's TajMahal is one of the most famous buildings in the world, the mausoleum of Shah Jahan's favorite wife, Mumtaz Mahal. It is one of the New Seven Wonders of the world, and one of three World Heritage Sites in Agra.

Jaipur/Udaipur

Jaipur is also popularly known as the Pink City, is the capital of the Indian state of Rajasthan. Jaipur is a very famous tourist and education Destination in India.

Goa

Goa is Famous for its pristine beaches, infact90% of all the tourism in Goa happens only for its beautiful beaches in Coastal Areas. Goa has two main tourist seasons: winter and summer. In the winter time, tourists from abroad (mainly Europe) come to Goa to enjoy the splendid climate. In the summertime (which, in Goa, is the rainy season), tourists from across India come to spend the holidays.

Kashmir

Kashmir was once called Heaven on Earth, and once of the most beautiful places in the world. However, in last couple of decades, terrorism has faded its charm-A place home to Himalayan Ranges.

Kanyakumari

Though there are several places of tourist interest in the town and district, Kanyakumari is especially popular in India for its spectacular and unique sunrise and sunset. The confluence of three ocean bodies-the Bay of Bengal, the Indian Ocean, and the Arabian Sea-makes the sunrise and sunset even more special. On balmy, full-moon evenings, one can also see the moon-rise and sunset at the same time-on either side of the horizon.

Kerala

Kerala, situated on the lush and tropical Malabar Coast, is **one of the most popular tourist destinations in India**. Named as one of the "**ten paradises of the world**" and "**50 places of a lifetime**" by the National Geographic Traveler magazine, Kerala is especially known for its ecotourism initiatives, Beautiful Backwaters and Alternative healing massages.

Old Delhi

Delhi, Capital of India has many attractions like mosques, forts and other monuments that represent India's history. The important places in Old Delhi include the majestic Red Fort. New Delhi on the other hand houses many government buildings and embassies, apart from places of historical interest. The QutubMinar, Red Fort and Humayun's Tomb have been declared World Heritage Sites.

Ajantha&Ellora

Ajantha&Ellora are 28-30 rock-cut cave monuments created during the first century BC and 5th century AD, containing paintings and sculptures considered to be masterpieces of both Buddhist religious art and universal pictorial art. The caves are located just outside the village of Ajantha/Ellora in Aurangabad district in the Indian state of Maharashtra. Since 1983, the Ajanta &Ellora Caves have been a UNESCO World Heritage Site.

Darjeeling

Darjeeling in India owes' its grandeur to its natural beauty, its clean fresh mountain air and above all, the smiling resilient people for whom it is a home. Known for its natural splendor, Darjeeling's best gift to its' visitors is the dawn of a new day. The mountains awaken first with a tentative peeking of the sun.

Mysore

Mysore is a tourism hot spot within the state of Karnataka and also acts as a base for other tourist places in the vicinity of the city. The city receives the maximum number of tourists during the period of the Dasara festival when festivities take place for a period of 10 days. One of the most visited monuments in India, the Ambavilas Palace (also known as Mysore Palace) is the center of the Dasara festivities.

LehLadakh

The Ladakh capital city of Leh lies near the eastern parts of Jammu and Kashmir, on the crossroads of the historic "Silk Route" from Sinkiang to West Asia and to the plains of India. The humbling monasteries of Shey, Hemis, Alchi, Thikse and Lamayuru will nurture your spiritual needs, and the landscape of Leh provides for a number of adventure activities including mountaineering, white-water rafting and trekking along the Markh Valley.

Gangtok

The capital of the state of Sikkim, Gangtok is an attractive tourist destination, reflecting a unique ambience which derives from its happy blend of tradition and modernity. Alongside the deeply felt presence of stupas and monasteries, Gangtok also bustles like any other thriving town. Some of the key places to visit include Rumtek Monastery, Do-DrulChorten, Enchey Monastery, Tashi View Point and the local bazaar, Lal Bazaar.

Seasonality in Tourism

Tourism is one of the biggest and fasted growing industries in the world, but it is characterised by seasonality. Tourism as an integral part of global business is highly dependent on seasonal changes in climatic conditions, economic activities as well as human behaviour and the society in general. Seasonality has become one of the most distinctive and determinative features of global tourism industry. The most significant aspect of seasonality is that it involves the concentration of tourist flows in relatively short periods of the year.

The concept of seasonality may be perceived to be familiar to many; however, there is no unique and precise definition of it. Season is "the most important period within the year, in which some certain things are bounding". It also refers to the existence of unevenness or fluctuation during the course of the year, which occurs in relation to a specific season.

Seasonality as 'a temporal imbalance in the phenomenon of tourism, which may be expressed in terms of dimensions of such elements as numbers of visitors, expenditure of visitors, traffic on highways and other forms of transportation, employment, and admissions to attractions'. Seasonality in tourism activity is not a particular characteristic of a single destination or country, as it is experienced in almost all countries and destinations in the world. Seasonality causes the fluctuation in tourists and visitor numbers to a destination. Therefore, some destinations at certain times have more tourists and visitors than they are able to accommodate, while at other times, there are too few tourists and visitors to the region.

Seasonality affects all aspects of supply-side behavior, finance, labor and stakeholder operations. The majority of the tourist operators dealing with the issue of seasonality identifies these systematic demand fluctuations as a problem, which has to be overcome or, at least, modified and reduced in effect. A good understanding of seasonality in tourism is essential for the efficient operation of tourism facilities and infrastructure.

Causes of Seasonality

1. Natural Causes
2. Institutional Causes
3. Additional Causes

Natural Causes of Seasonality

Natural seasonality, as the name implies, relates to regular and recurring temporal variations in natural phenomena, particularly those associated with climate and the seasons of the year including air temperature, water temperature, sunlight, snowfall, rainfall, extreme temperature, daylight, humidity, wind and geographical location (costal, alpine, urban, peripheral regions).

Natural seasonality associates with annual seasons and especially affects remote and peripheral destinations with big temperature differences between the seasons. Destinations with warm and cold climate are exposed to seasonal changes, due to different activities offered for tourists depending on climate and season.

Institutional Causes of Seasonality

Institutionalized seasonality is more complex as it is based on human behavior and consumer decision making (e.g. deciding on the timing of holidays) and results from religious, social, cultural, ethnic and organizational factors and policies. Institutionalized seasonality include: holidays (school, university, work, public, religious) and sociological and economic factors. Institutional factors reflect the social norms and practices of society. Unlike the natural seasonality, dates of institutionalized seasonality can be established more precise, as it often corresponds with school or public holidays, religious events or pilgrimage, celebration or conduction of various events and festivals, etc.

Additional Causes of Seasonality

In addition to natural and institutional seasonality, some other causes could be considered: Hosting time of sporting event. E.g. the Olympic Games World Cup, and Commonwealth Games. Sporting season-hunting season, skiing, surfing or golf. These activities require a combination of climatic and physical factors, along with the necessary infrastructure. Inertia, tradition and travel habits of travelers continue to travel at a specific time of the year even though they are no longer restricted to this particular period. Many people take holidays at peak seasons because they have always done so, and old habits tend to die hard.

Foreign Exchange Earnings

i. Foreign exchange earnings are profits made from selling goods and services in a global marketplace. In some cases, currency is simply exchanged in order to make these earnings without goods or services being sold. These earnings come in the currency of the country where the products or services are sold, so they have to be exchanged in order to be calculated. Many businesses make large amounts of money from foreign exchange earnings, so this marketplace, known as the Forex market.

ii. Foreign Exchange Earnings from tourism are the receipts of the country as a result of consumption expenditure, i.e. payments made for goods and services acquired, by foreign visitors in the economy out of the foreign currency brought by them. FEEs during the month of December 2014 were Rs 12,875 crore as compared to Rs 11,994 crore in December 2013 and Rs 10,549 crore in December 2012.The growth rate in FEEs in rupee terms in December 2014 over December 2013 was 7.3%.

iii. FEEs from tourism in rupee terms during January-December 2014 were Rs 1,20,083 crore with a growth of 11.5%, as compared to the FEE of Rs 1,07,671 crore with a growth of 14.0% during January- December 2013 over the corresponding period of 2012.

Visitor Profile

Analyzing Tourism Statistics

Researches in different scales are usually conducted by the government and other organizations with the objective of identifying certain patterns about the local tourism trends. Some common visitor statistics include the followings:

i. Visitor arrivals by major market areas.

ii. Total expenditure associated to inbound tourism.

iii. Purpose of visit.

iv. Places visited.

v. Overnight & same-day visitor arrivals.

vi. Visitor spending patterns.

vii. Average length of stay.

viii. Main items bought, etc.

According to "Visitor Profile Report2011" and "Tourism Review 2011" some key characteristics of visitors can be observed through the following:

i. **Purpose of Visit:** The main purpose of visit for overnight visitor is on vacation, followed by 'visiting friends and relatives' and 'business/meetings'.

ii. **Overnight Visitor Spending Patterns:** Visitors spend their money on accommodation, shopping, tours, meals outside hotels, entertainment and others. Among all these expenditures, overnight visitors spend most of their money (59.3%) on shopping.

iii.   **Same-day In-town Visitor Spending Patterns:** Same-day In-town visitor has a similar spending pattern, **Shopping Hotel Bills Meals Outside Hotels Others** shopping tops their total expenditures.

iv.   **Main Items Bought by Visitors:** Top Ten Main Items Bought by Visitors Ready-made. Wear, Cosmetics/Skin-care Products, Snacks/Confectioneries, Shoes/Other Footwear, Handbag/Wallets/Belts, Souvenirs/Handicrafts Medicine/Chinese Herbs, Perfume, Personal Care, Gold Jewellery, without Stone.

v.   **Places Visited by Visitors:** Based on the statistics, man-made attractions in particular shopping is the main pulling factor that influences visitors.

Factors Influencing the Growth of Tourism

The following image depicts the factors influencing the growth of tourism.

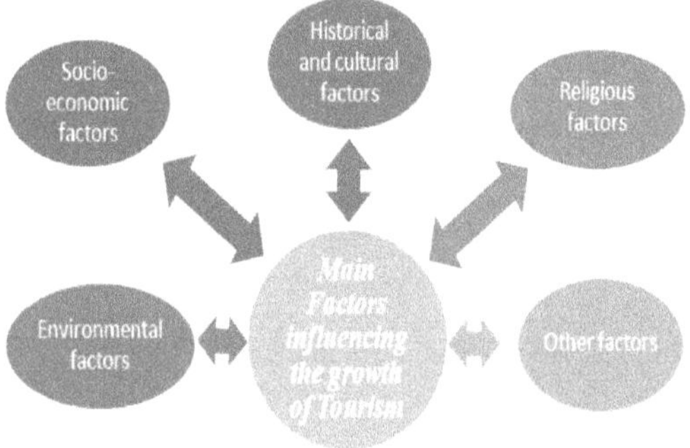

i.   *Environmental Factors*

- Good climate.
- Beautiful scenery, etc.

ii.   *Socio-economic Factors*

- Accessibility,
- Accommodation,
- Amenities,
- Ancillary services, etc.

iii.   *Historical and cultural factors.*

iv.   *Religious factors and*

v.   *Other factors.*

i. *Environmental Factors*

Two main environmental factors that have led to the growth of tourism:

- **Good Climate:** Good climate is one of the most important features of attraction for any tourist place. Pleasant climate with warmth and ample of sunshine attracts tourists who come from the temperate and colder regions.
- **Beautiful Scenery:** Tourism booms at picnic spots with beautiful sceneries. For example, sunrise and sunset points, long sea beaches, fresh water lakes, water falls, etc., often attract large numbers of tourists.

ii. *Socio-economic Factors*

Four important socio-economic factors that influence the development of tourism:

- **Accessibility:** Of all socio-economic factors, accessibility is the most important one. All tourist centers must be easily accessible by various modes of transportation like roads, railways, air and water.
- **Accommodation:** Places of tourists' interest must be capable enough to provide good accommodation and catering facilities. A type of accommodation required by tourists depends on their lives-styles, standard of living, capacity to spend money, nature of services expected, etc.
- **Amenities :** Growth of tourism at a particular place is also influenced crucial factors like; how well the site is maintained for touring activities like skiing, roping, paragliding, rowing, fishing, surfing, safari adventure, etc. Whether emergency facilities are available or not, so on.
- **Ancillary Services**: If a tour destination is equipped by ancillary (supplementary) services like banking and finance, the Internet and telecom connectivity, hospitals, insurance, so on, then such a place succeeds to hold (retain) more tourists for a longer time. This overall helps to boost the local economy to some extent.

iii. *Historical and Cultural Factors*

Many tourists are attracted to places of historical significance and that which have a legacy of rich cultural heritage. People love and enjoy exploring destinations where there are famous ancient monuments, marvelous forts, castles and palaces of earlier kings and queens, etc.

iv.   *Religious Factors*

People often make pilgrims to places of religious importance to seek inner peace, get blessing of their favorite deities and gurus, attain salvation before death, etc. Here, faiths, beliefs and sentiments of people contribute in booming tourism at holy places.

v.   *Other Factors*

Sometimes other factors also contribute toward growth of tourism at unexpected places. Research activities and adventures of deep seas and caves, geological studies of hot-water springs and geysers, seismic analysis of active volcanoes, investigation of paranormal-activities in abandoned ghost towns, etc. also contribute in developing tourism on some scale.

Impact of Tourism

The impacts of tourism can be sorted into seven general categories:

  i.   Economic
  ii.   Environmental
 iii.   Social and cultural
 iv.   Crowding and congestion
  v.   Services
 vi.   Taxes
vii.   Community attitude

i.   *Economic Impact*

The tourism industry generates substantial economic benefits to both host countries and tourists' home countries. Especially in developing countries, one of the primary motivations for a region to promote itself as a tourism destination is the expected economic improvement. Tourism increases employment opportunities. Additional jobs, ranging from low-wage entry-level to high-paying professional positions in management and technical fields, generate income and raise standards of living.

Particularly in rural areas, the diversification created by tourism helps communities that are possibly dependent on only one industry. As tourism grows, additional opportunities are created for investment, development, and infrastructure spending.

Tourism often induces in public utilities such as water, sewer, sidewalks, lighting, parking, public restrooms, litter control, and landscaping. Such improvements benefit tourists and residents alike. Likewise, tourism encourages improvements in transport infrastructure resulting in upgraded roads, airports, public transportation.

When considering the economic impacts of tourism, it is essential to understand that tourism businesses often include a significant number of low-paying jobs, often at minimum wage or less.

These jobs are often seasonal, causing under-employment or unemployment during off-seasons. Labour may be imported, rather than hired locally, especially if particular skills or expertise is required, or if local labour is unavailable.

Positive Impact

i. Contributes to income and standard of living
ii. Improves local economy
iii. Increases employment opportunities
iv. Improves investment, development, and infrastructure spending
v. Increases tax revenues
vi. Improves public utilities infrastructure
vii. Improves transport infrastructure
viii. Increases opportunities for shopping
ix. Economic impact (direct, indirect, induced spending) is widespread in the community
x. Creates new business opportunities

Negative Impact

i. Increases price of goods and services
ii. Increases price of land and housing
iii. Increases cost of living
iv. Increases potential for imported labor
v. Cost for additional infrastructure (water, sewer, power, fuel, medical, etc.)
vi. Increases road maintenance and transportation systems costs
vii. Seasonal tourism creates high-risk, under or unemployment issues
viii. Competition for land with other (higher- value) economic use
ix. Profits may be exported by non-local owners w Jobs may pay low wages

ii.   Environmental Impact

The quality of the environment, both natural and man-made, is essential to tourism. However, tourism's relationship with the environment is complex. It involves many activities that can have adverse environmental effects. Tourism has the potential to create beneficial effects on the environment by contributing to environmental protection and conservation. It is a way to raise awareness of environmental values and it can serve as a tool to finance protection of natural areas and increase their economic importance.

Areas with high-value natural resources, like oceans, lakes, waterfalls, mountains, unique flora and fauna, and great scenic beauty attract tourists and new residents (in-migrants) who seek emotional and spiritual connections with nature.

Positive Impact

i.   Protection of selected natural environments or prevention of further ecological decline

ii.   Preservation of historic buildings and monuments

iii. Improvement of the area's appearance (visual and aesthetic)

iv.   A "clean" industry (no smokestacks)

Negative Impact

i.   Pollution (air, water, noise, solid waste, and visual)

ii.   Loss of natural landscape and agricultural lands to tourism development

iii. Loss of open space

iv.   Destruction of flora and fauna (including collection of plants, animals, rocks, coral, or artifacts by or for tourists)

v.   Degradation of landscape, historic sites, and monuments

vi.   Water shortages

vii. Introduction of exotic species

viii. Disruption of wildlife breeding cycles and behaviours

iii.   Socio-Cultural Impact

The socio-cultural impacts of tourism are the effects on host communities of direct and indirect relations with tourists, and of interaction with the tourism industry. For a variety of reasons, host

Communities often are the weaker party in interactions with their guests and service providers. These influences are not always apparent, as they are difficult to measure, depend on value judgments and are often Indirect or hard to identify. Tourism can improve the quality of life in an area by increasing the number of attractions, recreational opportunities, and services. Tourism offers residents' opportunities to meet interesting people, make friendships, learn about the world, and expose themselves to new perspectives.

Positive Impact

i. Improves quality of life

ii. Facilitates meeting visitors (educational experience)

iii. Positive changes in values and customs

iv. Promotes cultural exchange

v. Improves understanding of different communities

vi. Preserves cultural identity of host population

vii. Increases demand for historical and cultural exhibits w Greater tolerance of social differences

viii. Satisfaction of psychological needs

Negative Impact

i. Excessive drinking, alcoholism, gambling

ii. Increased underage drinking w Crime, drugs, prostitution

iii. Increased smuggling

iv. Language and cultural effects

v. Unwanted lifestyle changes

vi. Displacement of residents for tourism development

vii. Negative changes in values and customs

viii. Family disruption

ix. Exclusion of locals from natural resources

x. New cliques modify social structure

xi. Natural, political, and public relations calamities

iv. Crowding and Congestion

People congregate in attractive places. Tourism often develops around specific locations and concentrates there, providing growth yet avoiding sprawl. Historic buildings and grounds, which might otherwise slowly deteriorate, have great appeal for tourism development and can often, are renovated to suit the industry.

Positive Impact

    i.   Minimizes sprawl

   ii.   Concentrates tourist facilities

  iii.   Old buildings reused for tourism

Negative Impact

    i.   Congestion including interference with other businesses

   ii.   Overcrowding-exceeding area capacity

  iii.   Conflict

  iv.   Overpowering building size and style

v.   *Services*

Tourism creates opportunities to develop new amenities and recreation facilities that wouldnot otherwise be viable in a community.

Positive Impact

    i.   Increases availability of recreation facilities and opportunities

   ii.   Better standard of services by shops, restaurants, and other commerce

  iii.   Improves quality of fire protection

  iv.   Improves quality of police protection

Negative Impact

    i.   Neglect of non-tourist recreation facilities

   ii.   Effects of competition

  iii.   Shortage of goods and services

  iv.   Increases pressure on infrastructure

vi.   *Taxes*

Increased retail activity from restaurants and tourist shopping will add state and local sales tax revenue. Lodging tax revenue to the city (or state) should increase since travellers account for virtually all lodging tax receipts. Increased tax burdens to expand infrastructure and public services will be passed on to property owners through increased property taxes.

Positive and Negative Impact

   i.   Additional state and local sales tax revenue

  ii.   Lodging tax revenue to city (or state)

 iii.   Increases property taxes

vii.   Community Attitude

Community Attitude Visitor interest and satisfaction in the community is a source of local pride.

Seeing visitor interest makes local residents more appreciative of local resources that are often taken for granted. As tourism develops, local residents will enjoy more facilities and a greater range of choices. Tourism activities and events tend to make living in a place more interesting and exciting.

Positive Impact

   i.   Heightens pride in community

  ii.   Greater appreciation of local resources

 iii.   More facilities and range of choices available

 iv.   More interesting and exciting place to live

Negative Impact

   i.   Heightens community divisiveness

  ii.   Increasingly hectic community and personal life

 iii.   Creates a phony folk culture

 iv.   Residents experience sense of exclusion and alienation over planning and development concerns

  v.   Feeling of loss of control over community future (caused by outsider development)

 vi.   New building styles fail to "fit" community

General Impacts

Generating Income and Employment: Tourism in India has emerged as an instrument of income and employment generation, poverty alleviation and sustainable human development. It contributes 6.23% to the national GDP and 8.78% of the total employment in India. Almost 20 million people are now working in the India's tourism industry.

Source of Foreign Exchange Earnings: Tourism is an important source of foreign exchange earnings in India. This has favourable impact on the balance of payment of the country. The tourism industry in India generated about US$100 billion in 2008 and that is expected to increase to US$275.5 billion by 2018 at a 9.4% annual growth rate.

Preservation of National Heritage and Environment: Tourism helps preserve several places which are of historical importance by declaring them as heritage sites. For instance, the TajMahal, the QutabMinar, Ajanta and Ellora temples, etc., would have been decayed and destroyed had it not been for the efforts taken by Tourism Department to preserve them. Likewise, tourism also helps in conserving the natural habitats of many endangered species.

Developing Infrastructure: Tourism tends to encourage the development of multiple-use infrastructure that benefits the host community, including various means of transports, health care facilities, and sports centres, in addition to the hotels and high-end restaurants that cater to foreign visitors. The development of infrastructure has in turn induced the development of other directly productive activities. Promoting Peace and Stability: Honey and Gilpin (2009) suggests that the tourism industry can also help promote peace and stability in developing country like India by providing jobs, generating income, diversifying the economy, protecting the environment, and promoting cross-cultural awareness. However, key challenges like adoption of regulatory frameworks, mechanisms to reduce crime and corruption, etc., must be addressed if peace-enhancing benefits from this industry are to be realized.

Unit-III

Activities of Department of Tourism

The department of tourism is Responsible for the promotion of India as a tourist destination and Development of Tourism Infrastructure facilities in the country. It is also performs Regulatory functions in the field of Tourism`

Activities

Promotional

It carriers out extensive publicity and promotion campaigns through its tourist offices located in the major tourist generating markets of the world viz: USA, Canada, UK, Western Europe, Australia, South, East Asia, Japan and West Asia.

Development

Various schemes under successive plans have been formulated and implemented for domestic and cultural Tourism, Development of Supplementary accommodation, promotion of wildlife tourism. Sports tourism, social, mountains and beach Resorts, promotion of fairs and Festivals grant of interest differential subsides for hostels, Grant loans for Tourist Transport Operations, leisure Tourism and Development of Travel Circuits.

Regulatory

It exercises the function of laying down norms and conditions for the operation of hotels, Travel agencies Tour operations and Tourist Transport operators and maintains approved list of the these agencies.

India Tourism Development Corporation (ITDC)

ITDC came into existence in October 1966 and has been the prime mover in the progressive development, promotion and expansion of tourism in the country.

The main objectives of the Corporation are:

- To construct, take over and manage existing hotels and market hotels, Beach Resorts, Travellers' Lodges/Restaurants.
- To provide transport, entertainment, shopping and conventional services.
- To produce, distribute tourist publicity material.

- To render consultancy-cum-managerial services in India and abroad.
- To carry on the business as Full-Fledged Money Changers (FFMC), restricted money changers etc.

To provide innovating, dependable and value for money solutions to the needs of tourism development and engineering industry including providing consultancy and project implementation.

The Corporation is running hotels, restaurants at various places for tourists, besides providing transport facilities. In addition, the Corporation is engaged in production, distribution and sale of tourist publicity literature and providing entertainment and duty free shopping facilities to the tourists. The Corporation has diversified into new avenues/ innovative services like Full-Fledged Money Changer (FFMC) services, engineering related consultancy services etc. The Ashok Institute of Hospitality & Tourism Management of the Corporation imparts training and education in the field of tourism and hospitality.

Presently, ITDC has a network of eight Ashok Group of Hotels, six Joint Venture Hotels, 2 Restaurants (including one Airport Restaurant), 12 Transport Units, One Tourist Service Station, 37 Duty Free Shops at International as well as Domestic Customs Airports, One Tax Free outlet and two Sound & Light Shows.

The Organization

The Ministry of Tourism is the nodal agency for the formulation of national policies and programmes and for the co-ordination of activities of various Central Government Agencies, State Governments/UTs and the Private Sector for the development and promotion of tourism in the country. This Ministry is headed by the Union Minister of State for Tourism (Independent Charge).The administrative head of the Ministry is the Secretary (Tourism). The Secretary also acts as the Director General (DG) Tourism. The office of the Director General of Tourism {now merged with the office of Secretary (Tourism)} provides executive directions for the implementation of various policies and programmes. Directorate General of Tourism has a field formation of 20 offices within the country and 14 offices abroad and one sub-ordinate office/project i.e. Indian Institute of Skiing and Mountaineering (IISM)/Gulmarg Winter Sports Project. The overseas offices are primarily responsible for tourism promotion and marketing in their respective areas and the field offices in India are responsible for providing information service to tourists and to monitor the progress of field projects. The activities of IISM/GWSP have now been revived and various Ski and other courses are being conducted in the J&K valley.

The Ministry of Tourism has under its charge a public sector undertaking, the India Tourism Development Corporation and the following autonomous institutions:

- Indian Institute of Tourism and Travel Management (IITTM) and National Institute of Water Sports (NIWS).
- National Council for Hotel Management and Catering Technology (NCHMCT) and the Institutes of Hotel Management.

Role and Functions of the Ministry of Tourism

The Ministry of Tourism functions as the nodal agency for the development of tourism in the country. It plays a crucial role in coordinating and supplementing the efforts of the State/Union Territory Governments, catalyzing private investment, strengthening promotional and marketing efforts and in providing trained manpower resources. The functions of the Ministry in this regard mainly consist of the following:

All Policy Matters, including:

- Development Policies.
- Incentives.
- External Assistance.
- Manpower Development.
- Promotion & Marketing.
- Investment Facilitation.

Functions of ITDC

Since ITDC is a Corporation that oversees many functions related to the Hospitality Sector. In its multi- functional role, ITDC aims at running all its units efficiently and productively and with improved margins of profit.

As the mainstay of the Hospitality Industry in India, ITDC plays a pivotal role in the creation and advancement of tourist infrastructure in India.

ITDC is a large Corporation under the Tourism Department of Government of India and carries a large number of employees in its different sections at various levels.

ITDC plays a vital role in getting together Government of each different State and its corresponding Tourism Development Corporation in planning and implementing new tourism-related projects, promotion of these projects, and training of required personnel.

A successful organization needs to have the correct ratio of man and work. ITDC works towards rationalizing size of the Human Resources so that the organization is trim and competent.

Shareholders who have put their trust in the organization should be adequately compensated by creating value for them.

Customers who are the backbone of any business venture should be provided with more than their money's worth so that they are satisfied and return for more.

Construction of new hotels and other hospitality related units, management of the existing ones and take-over of those hotels, motels, resorts, lodges and restaurants that are not doing well but have potential is one of the primary functions of the Corporation.

All other activities that are related to tourist facilities and interests such as transportation, entertainment, shopping, facilities for conventions and meetings etc. come in the purview of the functions of the Corporation.

Publicity matter related to tourism is envisioned, designed, produced and distributed by the Corporation.

ITDC also takes up consultancy and management of tourism related projects in the country and overseas.

Official money-changing facility for tourists, viz. Full-Fledged-Money-Changers (FFMC) and restricted money changers are also the functions of the Corporation.

Keeping tourism as the centre of focus, the Corporation provides innovative and viable answers to problems related to the Tourism and Engineering Industry.

Joint Venture Company of ITDC

ITDC works in tandem with State Tourism Development Corporations or State Tourism Departments in Joint Ventures that run properties that have now gained popularity and acclaim.

Name of the Joint Venture Company	Name of the Hotel property
Ranchi Ashok Bihar Hotel Corporation Ltd.	Hotel Ranchi Ashok, Ranchi
Utkal Ashok Hotel Corporation Ltd.	Hotel Nilachal Ashok, Puri
Donyi Polo Ashok Hotel Corporation Ltd.	Hotel Donyi Polo Ashok, Itanagar
Assam Ashok Hotel Corporation Ltd.	Hotel Brahmaputra Ashok, Guwahati
MP Ashok Hotel Corporation Ltd.	Hotel lake View Ashok, Bhopal
Pondicherry Ashok Hotel Corporation Ltd.	Hotel Pondicherry Ashok, Pondicherry
Punjab Ashok Hotel Company Ltd.	Hotel Anandpur Ashok, Anandpur (Project stage)

Divisions of ITDC

The main divisions of ITDC are:

- Hotels run under The Ashok Group brand
- Duty Free Shops
- Tour packages, Booking, Ticketing, Transportation under Ashok Tours and Travels
- Consultancy and Engineering Services
- Creation and distribution of Tourism related promotion material under the Ashok Creative brand
- Catering Units that operate canteens in New Delhi
- Vigyan Bhawan
- Western Court
- Hyderabad House
- Sound and Light Shows for tourists that tell the history of the monuments; Red Fort and Old Fort in Delhi
- Training and Education related to tourism through Ashok Institute of Hospitality & Tourism Management
- Event Management

State Tourism Development Corporation

The STDC (State Tourism Development Corporation): As practice in India almost every state has a state level corporation, which is given the task of development of tourism within the state.

Vision of STDC

To become one of the finest and leading service providers in the Hospitality Sector

Mission of STDC

To expand quality tourism infrastructure in the State and outside, in order to provide world class facilities to the tourists.

Objectives of the STDC are to

   (i) establish, develop, promote, execute, operate and otherwise carry on projects, schemes and other activities including running and maintenance of tourist vehicles to facilitate or accelerate the development of tourism;

   (ii) construct, run and maintain Tourist Information Bureaux and Centres in and outside the State within the Country;

   (iii) publish and sell different types of material for the purpose of giving publicity to tourism;

   (iv) Construct, lease out, take on lease, run and maintain tourist bungalows, tourist inns, youth hostels, hotels and cafeterias.

The other objectives are:

i. To promote as a leading tourist destination

ii. To identify key tourist destinations within and promote it outside

iii. To provide auxiliary support in developing key tourist destinations

iv. To provide highest quality hospitality services to tourists

v. To act as one-source destination for various information's regarding tourist destinations and other related information's.

vi. To ensure higher returns to government, through financial and social viable projects, and thereby provide employment

Role of STDC in Promotion of Tourism

i. A pioneer to initiate the tourism development process.

ii. Dispersal of tourism: expansion.

iii. Prime mover often without advantage: social mandate.

iv. Generate Employment.

v. Contribution to State revenue.

vi. Facilitated travel of tourists.

vii. Ensuring safe secure stay

viii. Official host of the Government

Tourism Planning

Planning is the dynamic process of determining goals, systematically selecting alternative courses of actions to achieve those goals, implementing the chosen alternatives and evaluating the choice to determine if it is successful. The planning process regards the environment which includes political, physical, social and economic elements as interrelated and interdependent components which should be taken into account in considering the future of a destination. Like any planning, tourism planning is goal-oriented, striving to achieve certain objectives by matching available resources and programs with the needs and wants of people. Comprehensive planning requires a systematic approach, usually involving a series of steps. The process is best viewed as an iterative and ongoing one, with each step subject to modification and refinement at any stage of the planning process.

Need for Tourism Planning

i. To determine the optimum level that can result in the achievement of environmental conservation objectives.

ii. To ensure that the natural and cultural resources are indefinitely maintained in the process of development.

iii. There must be careful matching of tourist markets and products through the panning process without compromising socio-cultural and environmental objectives.

iv. The direct and indirect economic benefits can be optimized through the careful and integrated planning.

v. Tourism can generate various socio-economic benefits as well as problems.

vi. Tourism is a multi-sectoral, complicated and fragmented activity such that planning and project development co-ordination are necessary.

vii. Planning provides the rational basis for development staging and project programming.

viii. To upgrade and revitalize existing outmoded or badly developed tourism areas and plan for new tourism areas in the future and

ix. To satisfy the manpower skis and capability requirements of tourism development.

Tourism Planning Process

The process of tourism planning involves:

i. Study recognition and preparation

ii. Setting of objectives or goals for the strategy

iii. Survey of existing data

iv.   Implementation of new surveys

v.   Analyses

vi.   Policy and plan formulation

vii.   Recommendation

viii.   Implementation of the plan

ix.   Monitoring and reformulation

Study Recognition and Preparation

Recognition by authorities that tourism is a desirable development option, together with some awareness of the contrasts within which it must develop.

Setting of Objectives or Goals for the Strategy

Have a clear understanding of the objectives that are to be achieved by the development of tourism.

Survey of Existing Data

Before setting out on the data collection stage, it is vital to undertake an existing data search.

Implementation of New Surveys

The data requirements for development planning are quite comprehensive and include:

i.   Tourism characteristics/travel patterns

ii.   Tourism attractions

iii.   Accommodation facilities

iv.   Other tourism facilities

v.   Land availability and use

vi.   Economic structure

vii.   Education and training needs and provisions

viii.   Environmental indicators

ix.   Socio-cultural characteristics

x.   Investment and available capital

xi.   Public and private sector organizations

xii.   Relevant legislation and regulations

Analyses

a. Asset evaluation- examining existing and potential stock assets

b. Market analysis

- Which market segments should be pursued?
- What kinds of tourism products and services should be provided?
- What kinds of promotion should be used?
- What prices should be charged for which products and services?

c. Development planning-phasing of development plan in order to ensure successful implementation

d. Impact Analyses

- Economic impacts
- Environmental impacts
- Socio-cultural impacts
- Impacts on local government
- Impacts on business and industry
- Impacts on residents

Policy and Plan Formulation

The results from the analyses of the survey data are unlike to yield a unique solution and instead will tend to suggest a number of possibilities for development strategies.

Recommendation

The preferred plan that has been selected on the basis of the analysis, having now been completed in detail, is submitted to the authorities by the planning team.

Implementation of the Plan

The methods of implementing the development plan will be considered throughout most stages of its construction.

Monitoring and Reformulation

Once the development plan has been implemented it must be closely monitored in order to detect any deviations that may occur from the projected path of development.

Unit-IV

Surface Transport

Surface transport means the movement of people or goods by road, train or ship. the movement of people or goods by road, train, or ship, rather than by plane.

Air Transport

In general, most of the airlines provide different classes of services on board; they are first, business and economy class. First-class travelers enjoy the privacy of their own private cabin area with plenty of good food, in-flight entertainment and personal video screen.

Business-class travelers have wide comfortable seats with plenty of legroom. They can also enjoy good food, free drinks, and complimentary newspapers.

Economy-class travelers though have narrower seats, still are provided with suitable services andmeals.

Besides, two types of flight are commonly seen in the market:

(i) Scheduled Flights

- Refer to those flights operated regularly according to a published timetables and fares.
- Irrespective to the number of passengers to be carried on any one flight, they serve on a

(ii) Non-scheduled Flights

- also known as charter flights
- do not operate on any set schedule or have predetermined fare structure
- Charter flights could go anywhere and at any time when scheduled service do not covered, and very often they supplement the service on regular routes during peak seasons.

Water Transport

Two common types of water transport are: cruise ships and ferry services.

i.   *Cruise Ships*

A cruise is a vacation trip by ship. This definition excludes travelling by water for primarily transportation purposes.

It offers the passengers a chance to relax in comfortable surroundings, with attentive service, good food, and a liner that changes the scenery from time to time.

Cruise ships are basically self-contained destinations where guests live, eat, are entertained, and travel. Cruises are voyages taken for pleasure and not only for the purpose of transport.

Most cruises start and end at the same port.

ii.   *Ferry Services*

Ferry service is a short distance sea-journey between ports. Both the local commuters as well as tourists use this mode of transport.

Road Transport

Traveling by road is the most flexible and economical form of mass transportation.

Modern motorway networks have made major cities easily accessible.

i.   Coach services

ii.   Car services

Rail Transport

The importance of rail travel has given way to private cars and air travel, but is picking up now since a number of services have been designed specifically for the tourist trade on a local and international level.

Mode	Carrying unit and capacity	Advantages	Disadvantages	Significance for tourism
Air	• Aircraft • Medium to High passenger capacity	• Speed and range • Suited to long distance journeys	• High fuel consumption • Stringent safety regulations make air transport an expensive mode	• Speed: shortened the travel distance and reduced the time of travel • Range: Increased accessibility to places, opened up most parts of the world for tourism. • Stimulate the growth of international mass tourism
Water	• Ship/cruise • Can have a high degree of comfort • Medium to High passenger capacity	• Suited to either long or short distance ferry operations • Relaxation	• Comparatively slow • Seasickness • High labourcos • Feeling of Confined while most of the activities limited in the cruise	Cruising became a popular form of leisure travel since 1980.
Road	• Car, bus, or coach. • Low capacity for passengers	• Door-to-door flexibility. • Suited to short distance journeys	Way shared by other users leading to possible congestion	• Door-to-door flexibility allows tourist to plan routes. • Allows carriage of holiday equipment. • Acts as a link between terminal and destination. • Acts as mass transport network for excursions in holiday areas
Rail	• Passenger carriages • High passenger capacity	• Convenience: it usually arrives at and depart from the central business district of a city, thus saving transit time between city and airport. • Suited to medium or long distance journeys, and to densely populated urban areas, • Environmental friendly	High fixed costs	In the mid-nineteenth century, it opened up areas previously inaccessible for tourism. • Special carriages can be added for scenic viewing, • Trans-continental routes and scenic lines carry significant volume of tourist traffic.

Airline Industry

Transport is a part of service and hospitality of a nation, this facility is very important for the movement of people to go somewhere. There are several mode of transportation such as road, rail, and water and also by air. All that kind of transportation is interplay each other to support the service and hospitality provided for tourist in that nation and the most suitable and relevant transport is air transportation. Airlines industry is a segment of travel industry that deals with air transportation from one destination to another destination.

Purpose of Travel

Normally people travel for various reasons, and in airlines world the purpose of people to travel can be classified into 4 types of travelers or reasons which are meeting, incentives, convention and exhibition (MICE). But there are other classifications such as business or work related education, leisure or holiday and visiting friends and relatives.

Influence of Air Transportation towards Tourism

Aviation provides the only worldwide transportation network, which makes it essential for global business and tourism. Air transportation alleviates poverty and helps to improve living standards by facilitating tourism. Air transport improves quality of life by broadening people's leisure and cultural experiences. It provides a wider choice of holiday destinations around the world and an affordable means to visit distance friends and relatives. Air transport contributes to sustainable development not only by facilitating tourism and trade, it generates economic growth, provides jobs, increase revenues from taxes as well as facilitates the delivery of emergency humanitarian aid relief and swift delivery of medical supplies anywhere on the earth. Air transportation promote safety and comfort in travel as it is being known as the safest mode of transportation. Furthermore, airlines provide hospitality for air traveller such as :

i. Modern and indulging facilities.

ii. High flexibility and accessibility

iii. Price for quality means you pay the tickets for the quality of service provided.

Due to economic crisis and increase in fuel price had affected airlines so much and this proportionally affecting the tourism industry.

Role of International Airlines in the Tourism Industry

The role of international airlines in the tourism business is to provide mass and quick transportation between countries under safe, standardized and economic conditions. Its relationship to the tourism industry is better understood by breaking down the entire activity of tourism into its component parts.

Purpose of Travel

Because of quick and efficient transportation, people are spurred to travel for various reasons as destinations have become more accessible. Some of these reasons to travel are:

i. Sightseeing-historical, cultural, social and technological sights.
ii. Relaxation-beach and mountain resorts.
iii. Sports-mountain climbing, skiing, surfing, scuba diving etc.
iv. Special interest-Study tours on art, history, religion, culture and science.
v. Shopping-personal and professional.
vi. Business.
vii. Governmental- political, cultural, social and scientific reasons.

The travel industry requires an efficient infrastructure which put together constitutes the tourism industry which is the world's second largest industry. The infrastructure is thus:

Transportation

Airlines (domestic and international); surface transportation such as shipping, rail, tour busses, rented cars, taxis, caravans, river transportation, etc.

Accommodation

Hotels of various categories* ranging from five star to modest unclassified hotels to meet all pockets. Motels which are modern 'inns' are situated on highways and provide garage facilities to keep transport safely.

Travel Agents

They put all the elements of the infrastructure together into one package.

Communications

Accessibility to destinations of interest by rail, road or air. Telecommunication systems to facilitate quick reservations, etc.

Other Services

Simple and quick formalities for entry into the country. Efficient baggage handling at airports, etc.

Freedom of the Air

Each country has a point of prestige its national carrier. To name a few, they are: Air India Of India, Lufthansa of West Germany, etc. There are basically six freedoms of the air:

i.   The right to overfly.

ii.   The right to make technical landing.

iii. The right to carry from one's own territory to another.

iv.   The right to carry from another territory to one's own.

v.   The right to carry between two territories.

vi.   The right to carry between two territories over one's own

Why has an Airline?

Governments have indulged themselves by running a national carrier irrespective of whether it is profitable or not. The reasons for this are many:

i.   Each government sees the potential of world tourism and wishes to take a slice of its revenue.

ii.   Having a national carrier is a source of price to each country.

iii. Sometimes due to political reasons government run airlines even though unprofitable

iv.   Airlines generate foreign exchange

v.   Airlines generate natural tourism growth.

Fares

Air fares are subjected to increasingly competitive conditions. For example, the world oil crisis has hit the airlines industry the maximum and many airlines have been liquidated or have had to cut down operations by reducing manpower and unprofitable routes. Together with recent world inflation and unemployment travel which came out of disposable income has become a luxury for a few. To meet such fluctuating world trends airlines have modulated their fares and devised novel methods of tariffs to meet the travel need of various segments.

They have thus come up with:

i. First class fares-for exclusive passengers.

ii. Economy fares-for the common passenger.

iii. Excursion fares-for students and emigrants.

All fares used by airlines come under two categories:

i. IATA fares.

ii. Government directed fares.

Types of packaged tours offered by airlines are:

i. Destination- where the ultimate destination is the unique selling point.

ii. Stop over packages-where a passenger has the benefit of stopping at other destinations lying en-route the ultimate destination.

iii. Special interest packages-sport, historical, etc.

iv. Brand name packages to destinations of known tourist attractions, e.g. Jet Tours, etc.

v. These packages guarantee value for money, backed by airlines name and reputation for maintenance of standards.

Travel Agency

A travel agency is a commercial enterprise where a traveler can secure information and expertise, get impartial counseling and make arrangements to travel by air, sea or land to any point in the world.

In other words a travel agency is an entity engaged in the business of extending to individuals or groups travel services and assistance to include documentations, ticketing, booking for transportation and/or accommodation arrangements, handling and/or conduct of tours within or outside the country whether or not for a fee, commission or any form of monetary consideration.

Travel Agent

A travel agent is one who acts as an agent for different suppliers or providers of products and services. He is one who engaged in selling and arranging transportation, accommodations, tours or trips for travelers.

Functions of Travel Agent

i.   Provides information and expertise

- How to get there?

- Where to stray?

- What to do?

ii.   Recommend destinations, products and services best suited to the needs of the client

iii.   Provide assistance in securing travel documents

iv.   Process travel arrangements

- Placing reservations

- Obtaining confirmation

- Determine package cost and inform

- Issuing ticket vouchers and other documents

- Monitoring the travel

v.   Assist in case of refunds and cancellations

The most important functions of a travel agency are described below:

1. Travel Information

A retail travel agency provides necessary travel information to the general public. The intending tourists come to the office of the travel agent and seek information regarding their proposed visit.

The travel agent should be a very knowledgeable man and should supply up to date and concrete information relating to travel.

He must have great communication skill and he should be thorough in the art of catching the potential customers. The knowledge of foreign language is a desirable qualification for those working in a travel agency.

2. Preparation of Itineraries

A tourist journey involves preparation of different types of itineraries. There are different means of transport with their respective advantages and disadvantages. A travel agent advises the potential tourist to choose the most convenient course.

3.   *Liaison with Providers of Service*

A travel agent should maintain constant contact with the providers of various services like the transport companies, hotel managers and providers of surface transport like motor cars from airport to hotel and for sightseeing etc.

Planning and Costing Tours

The contracts and arrangements having been entered into, there comes the task of planning and costing tours, both for inclusive programmes and to meet individual requirements. This job is intensely interesting and at the same time challenging.

This job calls for a great deal of initiative and drive. The job calls for travel to those places which are to be included in the itineraries.

This is essentially a job for a meticulously minded person and calls for considerable training and ability. Many agencies with the cooperation of airlines and other transportation companies take the opportunity of arranging educational tours for such staff to countries with which they deal.

Many agencies have people who are authorities on particular countries and, in addition to a general programme, many will issue separate programmes dealing with territories.

Separate programmes dealing with holiday offers based on specific forms of transportation, e.g., air, rail, road or sea, may also be prepared. Programmes also have to be issued to cover different seasons of the year.

Publicity is an important part of the programme. Having spent considerable time and money on preparing all that goes into the issue of a programme, publicity must feature considerably in the activities of a travel agency and more so if the agency happens to be a large one.

The majority of large travel agencies have their own publicity departments under the management of a publicity expert.

4.   *Ticketing*

Selling tickets to tourists for different modes of transport like air, rail and sea is a very important function of a travel agent. Ticketing is not an easy job as the range of international air fares is very complex. Computerised Reservation System (CRS) has revolutionised the reservation system both for air and train tickets and also a room in a hotel.

5. *Provision of Foreign Currencies*

Provision of foreign currency to an intending foreign tourist is an important function of a travel agent. The Government of India allows an Indian traveller going abroad 10,000 US $.

The travel agent will arrange for the purchase of foreign exchange on behalf of his intending travellers. This facility will save a lot of time and harassment for the intending tourists.

6. *Insurance*

Insurance for personal accident risks and risk for loss of baggage is an important function of a travel agent.

The idea of buying a package of travel, accommodation and perhaps some ancillary services such as entertainment became established in Western Europe in the 1960s. By 1970, tour operation had become a full-fledged part of tourism. Its growth was spectacular.

It succeeded in reducing the real price of travel abroad, in doing this; it brought holidays abroad to a segment of the market not reached by conventional methods of taking a holiday.

Today in most countries which are generators of tourism, tour operation is the dominating feature of the holiday market.

An inclusive tour is a package of transport and accommodation and perhaps some other services which are sold as a single holiday for a single all-inclusive price. The popular term, 'package holiday' describes the nature of a tour more accurately than the term 'inclusive tour'.

The original demand for inclusive arrangements came from the convenience of buying a single travel product.

Difference between Travel Agent and Tour Operator

Travel Agents	Tour Operator
Retailers	Wholesalers, Deals with Travel agents
Acts as consultants or advisers to the traveler	Acts as middlemen between the suppliers and the vendors
Revenues are fixed and pre-determined by suppliers	Have variable but limited revenues, income and profit margins
Charges fees for documentation and ancillary services	Sells optional products and services and make use of deposits

Computerized Reservation System

A computerized reservation system or central reservation system(CRS) is a computerized system used to store and retrieve information and conduct transactions related to air travel, hotels, car rental, or activities. Originally designed and operated by airlines, CRSs were later extended for the multiple airlines are known as global distribution systems (GDS). Modern GDSs typically allow users to book hotel rooms, rental cars, airline tickets as well as activities and tours. They also provide access to railway reservations and bus reservations in some markets.

What are CRS and GDS?

There have been 3 stages of evolution the first reservation system was called an Airline Reservation system, the second a Computer Reservation System (CRS) and the third evolution is today's Global Distribution System (GDS).

A computer Reservation System is a computerized system for saving and retrieving information when needed related to air travel. CRS were created and used by airlines and at a later point they were finally used in tourism in tourism intermediaries like travel agencies.

There is one downside of using GDS and it is the fact that it costs airlines money to go through a GDS process. Airlines complain that the prices are too high and therefore some poorer airlines have decided to post their best offers by using their own websites instead of the global distribution system.

CRS and GDS seem to have the same functions but the major difference between these two systems is that CRS only provide information about airlines whereas by using GDS you can reserve a ticket, a room in a hotel and also a rental car.

United Nations World Tourism Organization (UNWTO)

The United Nations World Tourism Organization (UNWTO) is the United Nations agency responsible for the promotion of responsible, sustainable and universally accessible tourism. It is the leading international organization in the field of tourism, which promotes tourism as a driver of economic growth, inclusive development and environmental sustainability and offers leadership and support to the sector in advancing knowledge and tourism policies worldwide. It encourages the implementation of the Global Code of Ethics for Tourism to maximize the contribution of tourism to socio-economic development, while minimizing its possible negative impacts, and is committed to promoting tourism as an instrument in achieving the United UNWTO generates market knowledge, promotes competitive and sustainable tourism policies and instruments, fosters tourism education and training, works to make tourism an effective tool. UNWTO's membership includes 156 countries, 6 territories and over 400 affiliate members representing the private sector, educational institutions, tourism associations and local tourism authorities. Its headquarters are located in Madrid, Spain.

The objectives of the UNWTO are to promote and develop sustainable tourism so as to contribute to economic development, international understanding, peace, prosperity and universal respect for, and observance of, human rights and fundamental freedoms for all, without distinction as to race, sex, language or religion. In pursuing these aims, UNWTO pays particular attention to the interests of developing countries in the field of tourism.

WTO Activities

Regional Representations and Programme Activity Sections of WTO work in the various fields of tourism. The knowledge and information generated are disseminated through publications, conferences, seminars, workshops and other meetings, as well as the WTO website.

Cooperation for Development

Acting on requests from Member Governments, WTO secures financing, locates the world's leading experts, and carries out all types of tourism development projects of small and large scales.

Statistics and Market Research

WTO is the world's most complete and reliable source of global and regional tourism statistics, economic analysis, market trends and forecasts.

Human Resources Development

In cooperation with its network of Education and Training Centers throughout the world, WTO sets global standards for tourism education

Quality of Tourism Development

Liberalization, health and safety reflect the broad and inter-connected range of issues related to improving the quality of tourism services. WTO is working towards the removal of barriers to tourism and is encouraging the liberalization of trade in tourism services, meanwhile respecting the principles of sustainable development.

Communications, Publication and Documentation

The Communications Section acts as a contact point and coordinator for press and media purposes. WTO has its own Publications Unit, its Documentation Centre houses a wide range of tourism research and information sources.

Sustainable Development of Tourism

In WTO's effort of generating know-how and disseminating information among its members and the international tourism community, the issues of sustainable development represent a high priority and its principles are applied in every WTO project.

International Air Transport Association (IATA)

The international Air Transport Association (IATA) was established in 1945 in order to promote safe, regular, and economical air transport. The members of IATA are individual international airlines.

Functions of IATA Include

- To act as a ticket clearing house; and
- To ensure the standardization of prices, tickets, and baggage checks.

The main role of IATA is coordinating international commercial airline industry activities and compromising on international airfares.

Other Activities

i. IATA assigns three-later and two-letter codes to airports and airlines, respectively, which are commonly used worldwide. IATO also assigns airport and airline codes. For Rail & Fly system, IATA also assigns IATA train station codes, IATA assigns IATA Delay Codes.

ii. IATA is pivotal in the worldwide accreditation of travel agents. In the U.S., agents who wish to sell airline tickets must also achieve accreditation with the Airlines Reporting Corporation.

iii. IATA administrates worldwide the Billing and Settlement Plan (BSP) and Cargo Accounts Settlement Systems (CASS) that serve as a facilitator of the sales.

iv. IATA regulates the shipping of dangerous goods and publishes the IATA Dangerous Goods Regulations manual (DGR) yearly.

v. IATA coordinates the scheduling process which governs the allocation and exchange of slots at congested airports worldwide, applying fair, transparent and non-discriminatory principles

vi.   IATA maintains the Timatic database containing cross border passenger documentation requirements. It is used by airlines to determine whether a passenger can be carried and helps travel agents to provide this information to travelers at the time of booking.

vii.   IATA publishes standards for use in the airline industry. The Bar Coded Boarding Pass (BCBP) standard defines the 2-dimensional (2D) bar code printed on paper boarding passes. The Electronic Miscellaneous Document (EMD) defines a standard document to account airlines sales and track usage of charges.

Hotel Industry

A hotel is an establishment that provides lodging paid on a short-term basis. The provision of basic accommodation, in times past, consisting only of a room with a bed, a cupboard, a small table and a washstand. Additional common features found in hotel rooms are a telephone, an alarm clock, a television, a bar with snack foods and drinks and facilities for making tea and coffee. Luxury features include bathrobes and slippers, a pillow menu, twin-sink vanities, and Jacuzzi bathtubs. Larger hotels may provide additional guest facilities such as a swimming pool, fitness center, business center, childcare, conference facilities and social function services.

Hotel rooms are usually numbered to allow guests to identify their room.

Accommodation Types

1. Guest House

A guest house normally has at least 4 letting bedrooms, some with ensuite or private facilities. It is usually run as a commercial business. Breakfast is available and evening meals may be provided.

2. B&B (Bed & Breakfast)

Accommodation offering bed and breakfast, usually in a private house. B&Bs normally accommodate no more than 6 guests, and may or may not serve an evening meal.

3. Small Hotel

A small hotel normally has a minimum of 6 bedrooms and a maximum of 20. Most bedrooms have private facilities. Small hotels serve breakfast, dinner and, normally, lunch, and they have a drinks licence.

4. Hotel

A hotel normally has at least 20 letting bedrooms, of which most have private facilities. They serve breakfast, dinner, and, normally, lunch, and they usually have a drinks licence.

5. International Resort Hotel

A hotel with a 5-star quality award that has a range of leisure and sporting facilities. These include an 18-hole golf course, swimming pool and leisure centre, and country pursuits.

6. Self-catering

A house, cottage, apartment, chalet or similar accommodation, with self-catering facilities, which is let normally on a weekly basis to individuals.

7. Serviced Apartment

Self-catering apartments where services such as cleaning are available. Meals and drinks may also be available, either to each apartment or in a restaurant and/or bar on site.

8. Lodge

Overnight accommodation, usually purpose built and situated close to a major road or city centre. Reception hours may be restricted and payment may be required on check-in. These may be associated restaurant facilities.

9. Inn

Bed and breakfast accommodation within a traditional inn or pub. The bar and restaurant is open to non-residents and provide in food at lunchtime and in the evening.

10. Restaurant With Rooms

The restaurant is the most significant part of the business, and is open to non-residents as well as those staying there. Breakfast is usually provided.

11. Campus Accommodation

The accommodation provided by colleges and universities for their students is often made available with meals to individuals or group at certain times of year.

12. Hotel

A building run by a private operator or non-profit membership organisation, where beds and sometimes meals and other services and facilities are provided.

13. Holiday Park

A park that offers holiday homes and, most likely, touring and camping pitches.

14. Touring Park

A park that offers touring pitches, and may offer camping pitches as well.

15. Camping Park

A park for camping only.

16. Motels

A motel is a hotel mainly for motorists and located conveniently near a major motorway.

Management Contract

A management contract is an agreement between a hotel owner and hotel management company under which, for a fee, the management company operates the hotel.

In a management agreement, the chain basically provides the same services as a franchise agreement, such as brand, reservation system etc., but on top of this, there is an agency agreement, meaning the brand operates the hotel, making all the day-to-day decisions on behalf of the owner.

The group names a general manager, who will generally come from its own system, or will hire and train one for the specific hotel; he or she will hire the staff, and will control costs and revenue, food costs, apply brand standards, and generally supervise the management of the hotel. The General Manager reports to the Regional Director, who in turn reports to the Regional Vice President, and there are daily and monthly reports. However the bank account and local management company still belong to the owner.

At the beginning of each financial year, a budget is prepared and presented to the owner. It presents the projected revenue and operating costs, and once the cost structure is established, the manager must stick to the budget.

Referral System

A system by which one hotel or restaurant recommends another, and may take bookings for another on which commission may be paid is called a referral system. A referral has the advantage of someone's experience attached to it.

Franchising

A hotel franchise is an agreement between a hotel chain (franchisor) and the hotel owner (franchisee), where the hotel chain allows the owner to make use of the chain's name and services In return; the owner pays the franchisor a fee for the franchise, which usually consists of various elements. The hotel chain has no ownership or financial interest in the hotel and is not directly responsible for the hotels results.

Franchise Terminology

Franchisor

The parent company that grants, for a fee and other considerations, the right to use its name and system of business operations is a franchisor.

Franchisee

The business partner, who invests his assets in a brand, operating system and ongoing support, is a franchisee.

Franchise Fee

An up-front entry fee, usually payable upon the signing of the franchise agreement for the right to use the franchisor's name, logo, and business system.

Royalty

A continuing payment to the franchisor that is payable on a periodic basis throughout the term of the franchise agreement.

Franchise Services

- Marketing and Advertising.
- Brand recognition.
- Reservation systems.
- Technology, soft – and hardware.
- Training.
- Design plans and specifications.
- Financing.
- Site selection and market analysis.
- PR and promotion support.
- Quality assurance programs.
- Purchasing.

Franchising fees

i.   The franchise fee is usually based on a fixed amount per room and has to be paid upon submission of the franchise application. This fee covers the franchisor's cost of processing the application, reviewing the site and market potential etc.,

ii. The royalty commences when the hotel assumes the franchise affiliation resp. starts its operation. This fee is usually paid monthly over the term of the franchise agreement.

iii. In addition fees may be due for loyalty programs, consulting, purchasing assistance, equipment rental etc.

Hotel Industry in India

'Hotel Industry in India' has supply of 1,10,000 rooms. According to the tourism ministry, 4.4 million tourists visited India last year and at current trend, demand will rise to 10 million in 2010 to accommodate 350 million domestic travelers. With tremendous pull of opportunity, India is a destination for hotel chins looking for growth. The World Travel and Tourism Council, India, data says, India ranks 18th in business travel and will be among the top 5 in this decade. Demand is going to exceed supply by at least 100% over the next 2 years Five star hotels in metro cities allot same room, more than once a day to different guests, receiving almost 24 hour rates from both guests against 6-8 hours usage. With demand supply disparity, 'Hotel India' room rates are most likely to rise 25% annually and occupancy to rise by 80% over the next two years.

India Hotel Industry' is adding about 60,000 quality rooms, in different stages of planning and development and should be ready by 2012. MNC Hotel Industry giants are flocking India and forging Joint Ventures to earn their share of pie in the race. Government has approved 30 hotel projects, nearly half of which are in the luxury range. Sources said the manpower requirements of the hotel industry will increase from 7 million in 2002 to 15 million by 2010.

Already, more than 50 international budget chains are moving into India to stake their turf. Therefore, with opportunities galore the future Scenario of India Hotel Industry' looks rosy.

Indian tourism and hospitality sector has reached new heights today. Travelers are taking new interests in the country which leads to the upgrading of the hospitality sector. Even an increase in business travel has driven the hospitality sector to serve their guests better. Visiting foreigners has reached a record 3.92 million and consequently International tourism receipts have also reached a height of US$ 5.7 billion.

Hospitality Industry is closely linked with travel and tourism industries. India is experiencing huge footfalls as a favorite vacation destination of foreigners and natives and the hospitality industry is going into a tizzy working towards improving itself. Fierce competition and fight to rank on the number one position is leading the leaders of this industry to contemplate on ideas and innovate successful hospitality products and services every day.

    i.   The Grand Ashok–Bangalore.

   ii.   International the Grand Resort–Goa.

  iii.   The Grand Palace–Srinagar.

  iv.   The Grand Laxmi Vilas Palace–Udaipur.

   v.   The Grand Temple View–Khajuraho.

Major Hotel Chains of India

Taj Group

The group of hotels is one of the finest five star hotels in India. The group has luxury boutique hotels combines' classic heritage with modern elegance and luxury. Some of the most wonderful hotels of the Taj Group include the Taj View Hotel at Agra, Taj Residency at Aurangabad, Taj Coromandel in Chennai, Taj Bengal at Kolkata and the Taj President at Mumbai.

The ITDC Ashok Group of Hotels

The ITDC Ashok Group of Hotels are said to be ones who pioneered the India Hotel industry. The ITDC Ashok Group of Hotels owns 33 hotels in 26 destinations across India.

Some of the hotels of the ITDC Ashok Group in India are:

- The Ashok, Delhi.
- The Samrat Hotel, Delhi.
- LalithaMahal Palace, Mysore.
- Hotel Jaipur Ashok, Jaipur.
- Hotel Janpath, Delhi.
- Ranchi Ashok, Ranchi.
- Hotel Jammu Ashok, Jammu.

Oberoi Group

The Oberoi group is an epitome of luxury and hospitality. The Group was founded in 1934 and is now one of the largest Hotel group in India. Some of the wonderful hotels of this group include the oberoi Grand at Kolkata, oberoi Amar Vilas at Agra, The Oberoi at Mumbai, Oberoi Rajvilas at Jaipur and the Oberoi Cecil at Shimla.

ITC Welcome Group

This group has over 70 hotels across the country. Some of the major hotels of this group include the Rama International at Aurangabad, Grand Bay at Visakhapatnam, ITC Sonar Bangla in Kolkata and the ITC Kakatiya at Hyderabad.

The Le Meridien Group Of Hotels

The Le Merdien Group of Hotels is a luxury hotel group established in 1972. There are more than 130 luxury Le Meridien hotels in more than 53 countries of the world.

Some of the hotels of the Le Meridien Group in India are:

- Le Meridien, Ahmedabad.
- Le Meridien, Bangalore.
- Le Meridien, New Delhi.
- Le Meridien, Pune.
- The Metropolitan Hotel Nikko, New Delhi.

Best Western Group of Hotels

The Beat Western Group is the largest hotel chain of the world with over 4,000 hotels in more than 80 countries. This hotel chain has a series of hotels that spread near leading tourism and business destinations.

Some of the hotels of Best Western Group are:

- Best Western Anand palace, Dharamshala.
- Best Western RadhaAshok, Mathura.
- Best Western OM Towers, Jaipur.
- Best Western Germanus, Madurai.
- Best Western pleasant Days, Chennai.
- Best Western The Pride Hotel, Pune.

The Grand International

The Grand International group of hotels is a collaboration of two industries-The International Intercontinental Group of Hotels and the Indian The Grand Group of hotels. The former is a leading hotel chain of the world with nearly 3500 hotels spread in more than 100 countries, while the latter is an enterprise of Bharat Hotels Ltd.

Some of the hotels of The Grand International in India are:

- Intercontinental The Grand–Mumbai

Promotion of Tourism in India

Incredible India Campaign

The Indian Ministry of Tourism launched the Incredible India campaign in 2002 to encourage visitors from around the world to experience India.

More Lodging Available

The Ministry of Tourism has encouraged Indian entrepreneurs to start hosting tourists in bed and breakfast style guest lodging. These B&Bs offer visitors the Indian cuisine, culture and people, and a number of guest rooms available in metropolitan areas.

Transportation and Accessibility

The Indian government is allocating funds to improve the infrastructure of the nation. One such improvement has been the installation of heliports, where visitors can easily travel from a major metropolitan area to a rural area by helicopter.

Heritage & Ecotourism

A popular heritage site is the TajMahal, which attracts millions of visitors each year. The Ministry is integrating the ideas of conservation and preservation of the local ecology and culture to the greatest extent possible.

Health and Wellness Tourism

As the birthplace of yoga and Ayurveda, the Ministry used to highlight these traditions in their campaigns.

Participation in Travel Fairs and Exhibitions

India Tourism officers overseas have participated in the major International Travel Fairs and Exhibitions in important tourist generating markets all over the world.

i.   Road shows were organized in important tourist generating markets overseas with participation of different segments of the travel industry.

Importance of Tourism Promotion

1.   Economic Benefits

i) Increasing Job Opportunities

Employment may be associated directly, such as tour guide or managerial positions; or in supporting industries like food production or retail suppliers.

ii) Increased Spending

Increased spending in the community generated from visitors or tourism businesses can directly and indirectly promote the visibility of local businesses.

iii) Economic Diversification

By offering an additional means of income, tourism can support a community when a traditional industry is under financial pressure.

iv) Infrastructure Improvement

Infrastructure including roads, parks, and other public spaces can be developed and improved both for visitors and local residents.

2.   Social Benefits

Community identify and pride can be generated through tourism. A positive sense of community identity can be reinforced and tourism can encourage local communities to maintain their traditions and identity.

3.   Environmental Benefits

Providing financial or in kind support for the conservation of the local environment and natural resources will enhance the reputation of any tourism business.

Tourism Advertising

Advertising is a paid form of non-personal presentation of a product or service by an identified sponsor. It has three aims; first it sells potential customers of the existing product or service and the benefits expected to accrue from its possession or se; second, it reminds customers of its continued existence to obtain repeat business and third, it seeks to regain lost customers who may have switched to other suppliers.

The advertising is aimed at the public to create awareness of the travel offers available, or a resort and its attractions to influence their business decisions. The media available for advertising are newspapers, technical press, commercial television, commercial radio, poster sites, cinema and theatres. Advertising in tourism essentially follows the AIDA principles of attracting attention, creating awareness, fostering desire and inspiring action.

Advertisings and Its Role on Tourism

In the tourism industry, the products are destination, accommodation, transportation etc. The advertisement can be made in newspapers, general and special magazines, especially in the form of posters or bill boards. Advertisement spreads information amongst the potential tourists about the particular resort or hotel or airline or other transportation services to and fro the tourist sites. This offers to the prospects an opportunity of making choice. The sensitive slogans beat the efficacy on influencing the travelling decisions. Television has made possible multi-dimensional display of advertisements which is impossible through other tools of promotion. This adds attraction to the destination and becomes successful in creating interests. The multi-faceted facilities offered by hotels and airlines can be well informed to the potential travelers. Therefore, advertising is the means by which the necessary information is given on tourist and tourist areas, used to convince them to travel. In fact, advertising is includes taking advantage of the written media (Video and Audio) to send the message to different consumers in travel and tourism, with the aim of getting an immediate response from the consumer market.

Tourism Publicity

Publicity another dimension of promotion known as an unpaid form of persuasive communication also plays an incremental role in promoting the hotel business. While publicizing, the hotel professionals play a significant role by managing the media personnel or publishing news items related to the hotel.

In the public relations, the activities range from a press release to' newspapers and magazines, especially to create the interest of prospects in a holiday package in a good resort of a country. The holiday package tours and trips on familiarity with a tour spot, organised by tour operators for the travel agents help them in enriching their knowledge and making the travelling decisions.

Public relations activities thus become instrumental in the process of publicizing. The tourism publicity plays a crucial role in attracting tourists and promoting tourism.

The publicity programme include regular publicity, stories and photographs to the newspapers, travel editors, contact with magazines on stories, ideas and the framing of story outlines and pictures etc. In the hotel industry, public relations activities are more instrumental in informing the clients the outstanding merits of different services offered. The specialties of hotel are presented in such a way that the prospects are motivated to avail of the facilities offered by a particular hotel- It also helps in creating an atmosphere where the users at large are convinced. Besides, it also helps in collecting the information on the preferences of the prospects. There are a number of media sources available for publicity. Illustration, copy and the spoken word are the primary publicity to media which are grouped into the following heads:

i.   Printed publicity
ii. Advertising publicity
iii. Projected publicity
iv. Structural publicity
v.   Personal publicity

The 'illustration' is found helpful in achieving emotional effects, the 'copy' give expression to the publicity idea and the 'spoken word' found important in the case of personal publicity. Thus it is right to say that public relations activities occupy a significant place in the promotion mix of hotel companies.

References

1. J.M.S. Negi, "Travel Agency and Tour Operation, Concepts and Principles", Kanishka Publishers, 2009.

2. Mohinder Chand, "Travel Agency and Tour Operation-An introductory Text", Anmol Publishers, 2010.

3. "Negi: Professional Hotel Management", Delhi: S. Chand.

4. Zeithaml VA, "Service Marketing", McGraw Hill, London, 1996.

5. A.K. Bhatia, "Basics of Tourism Management", Sterling Publishers Pvt Delhi, 2010

6. A.G. Krishna, "Case study on the effects of tourism on culture and the environment", Jaisalmer, Khajuraho and Goa, 1993.

7. Honey, Martha and Gilpin, Raymond, Special Report, "Tourism in the Developing World-Promoting Peace and Reducing Poverty", 2009.

8. Market Research Division, Ministry of tourism, GOI, 2009 "Tourism Statistics 2008"

9. www.ibef.org

10. www.incredibleindia.org

11. http://en.wikipedia.org/wiki/Tourism

12. http://www.gdrc.org/uem/eco-tour/envi/index.html

13. http://booksgoogle.co.in

14. www.sciencedirect.com

www.ingramcontent.com/pod-product-compliance
Lightning Source LLC
Chambersburg PA
CBHW051131160726
47997CB00018B/1151